KT-382-319

✺ INSIGHT COMPACT GUIDE

COPENHAGEN

Compact Guide: Copenhagen is the ultimate quick-reference guide to this fascinating destination. It tells you all you need to know about Denmark's lively capital. From the Changing of the Guard at the royal palaces to the fun of the Tivoli Gardens, from the elegant designer shopping of Strøget to the radical lifestyles of Christiania, it's all here.

This is one of 133 Compact Guides produced by the editors of Insight Guides, whose books have set the standard for visual travel guides since 1970. Packed with information, arranged in easy-to-follow routes, and lavishly illustrated with photographs, this book not only steers you round Copenhagen but also gives you fascinating insights into local life.

Discovery
CHANNEL

APA PUBLICATIONS
Part of the Langenscheidt Publishing Group

Insight Compact Guide: Copenhagen

Written by: Alexander Geh
English version by: Paul Fletcher
Updated by: Rachel Gravesen
Main photography and cover picture by: Jerry Dennis
Additional photography by: Jeroen Snijders; AKG London 96/1, 103,
106/1; Courtesy Carlsberg 31/2; Courtesy Danish Tourist Board 24/2, 41/2,
64/1, 66/1, 99/2; Courtesy Faerdighoe 30; Ronald Grant Archive 106/2,
108; Rudy Hemmingsen/Apa 80/2, 81; Topham Picturepoint 12/1, 105/1
Design: Graham Mitchener
Picture Editor: Hilary Genin
Maps: Polyglott/Rachfall
Design concept: Carlotta Junger

Editorial Director: Brian Bell
Managing Editor: Tony Halliday

CONTACTING THE EDITORS: As every effort is made to provide accurate
information in this publication, we would appreciate it if readers would
call our attention to any errors and omissions by contacting:
Apa Publications, PO Box 7910, London SE1 1WE, England.
Fax: (44 20) 7403 0290
e-mail: insight@apaguide.co.uk

Information has been obtained from sources believed to be reliable,
but its accuracy and completeness, and the opinions based thereon,
are not guaranteed.

© 2006 APA Publications GmbH & Co. Verlag KG Singapore Branch, Singapore.

Second Edition 2002; Updated 2005; Reprinted 2006
Printed in Singapore by Insight Print Services (Pte) Ltd

Worldwide distribution enquiries:
APA Publications GmbH & Co. Verlag KG (Singapore Branch)
38 Joo Koon Road, Singapore 628990
Tel: (65) 6865-1600, Fax: (65) 6861-6438

Distributed in the UK & Ireland by:
GeoCenter International Ltd
Meridian House, Churchill Way West, Basingstoke,
Hampshire RG21 6YR
Fax: (44 1256) 817-988

Distributed in the United States by:
Langenscheidt Publishers, Inc.
36-36 33rd Street 4th Floor
Long Island City, New York 11106

www.insightguides.com
In North America:
www.insighttravelguides.co

Introduction

Places

Culture

Travel Tips

▷ **Christiania p79**
This 'free state', a bold experiment in communal living and self-government, is a hotbed of creativity.

▽ **Slotsholmen p36**
The historic centre of the city is home to some magnificent architecture.

▷ **Amalienborg p60**
The royal palace at Amalienborg is the setting for the changing of the royal guard, so time your visit to see this display of military precision.

▷ **Roskilde p99**
One of Denmark's oldest towns and the burial place for the country's monarchs.

▽ **Louisiana Museum for Moderne Kunst p97**
One of the world's best collections of modern art.

▷ **Rosenburg Slot p55**
This 17th-century palace has a fabulous collection of furniture, paintings and, above all, houses the Danish crown jewels.

△ **Carlsberg p31**
The Carlsberg Brewery is a well-loved institution in this city of beer drinkers.

△ **Nationalmuseet p35**
A huge and eclectic collection of artefacts from many different periods of history and cultures, with excellent facilities for children.

Tivoli p22
e Tivoli pleasure gardens e famous the world over. well as the floral splays, there are rides d many cultural events.

▷ **Nyhavn p65**
Copenhagen's revamped docks cater to a different clientele these days but are still a lively area full of bars and surrounded by boats.

Scandinavia's Liveliest Capital

When Denmark briefly ruled all of Scandinavia, Copenhagen was the capital of Norway and Sweden as well. The Danes still like to regard their capital as the region's most important and cosmopolitan city.

Copenhagen occupies a delightful spot by the Øresund; the waters of this narrow link between the Baltic and the Kattegat flow right past the heart of the city via a series of man-made canals and natural channels. Although most of the docks and quayside installations have gone for good, the maritime atmosphere is ever-present; indeed the best way to get a first feel of the city is from the water. But Copenhagen is also very much a walking city, the first European capital to be developed with an understanding of the pleasure of strolling through streets free of motor cars and exhaust fumes.

Below: Nyhavn waterfront
Bottom: Rådhusplasden

INFORMAL ATMOSPHERE
The casual pace of the crowds extends to the city's delightful parks and open spaces – favoured venues for picnics and recreation. Children and young people are not restricted by signs and by-laws and adults appreciate the informality that is so much a part of the Danish character. In fact, it is the friendliness and openness of the Copenhageners that has helped to make the city so popular as a holiday destination.

SPIRITED CULTURAL SCENE
Copenhagen's varied cultural calendar has something for everyone: paintings and sculptures for the art enthusiast, avant-garde and alternative lifestyles for the younger generation, and the fairy tales of Hans Christian Andersen for children. Whether it is classical music or rock music, art or literature, museums or open-air sculpture that draws you to Copenhagen, the choice is broad.

Few would dispute that Copenhagen is the liveliest of the Scandinavian capitals, with some-

Opposite: the Little Mermaid

Population
The population of Copenhagen is about 502,000, and the separate entity of Frederiksberg has a population of over 91,000. When you add in the outlying suburbs, greater Copenhagen's numbers rise to around 1.77 million.

Exploring the city

thing going on every day and night. It would be a shame to try to cram everything that this wonderful city has to offer into a weekend. Try to allow a few more days to savour its intriguing mixture of big-city jungle and quiet backwaters.

LOCATION

The Danish capital is located on the 55th parallel at about the same distance from the equator as Glasgow and Moscow. Copenhagen lies on the eastern side of the Baltic Sjælland island and on the islands Sjælland and Amager. The Øresund is about 16km (10 miles) wide at this point and separates Sjælland and Amager in the west from the Swedish mainland in the east. From earliest times, the Sund has been the main waterway between the Baltic and the Kattegat.

CLIMATE AND WHEN TO GO

A maritime position in a temperate climate zone generally means stable temperatures but changing weather patterns. A week of unbroken sunshine is rare, but that is actually more likely than seven days of persistent rain. Light rainwear is always advisable, with umbrellas often unsuitable in the strong winds.

If you want to explore Copenhagen's open spaces and take lots of walks around the city, then you can rely on warm or at least adequate temperatures from May through to September.

Museums and indoor entertainment in the capital can be enjoyed at any time of the year. But outdoor types need not necessarily shun the wet and windy months from November onwards. Tourists are few and far between during the winter and accommodation tends to be cheaper.

THE LANGUAGE

Foreigners who make an attempt to speak the language of their hosts are always well received. However, the Danes speak very

quickly and often drop not only letters but also syllables, so well-meaning but inexperienced tourists, after having been asked a simple question in a café three times, may well abandon their attempts to emulate the natives. Most Danes can, after all, make themselves understood perfectly well in English. Despite these pronunciation difficulties, saying the little word *tak* ('thank you') is always appreciated.

The Danish language has some letters of its own: Æ and æ correspond roughly with 'e' as in 'end', Ø and ø with 'er' in 'fern', Å and å (sometimes written as 'Aa' or 'aa') is a long, open sound. *(For a selection of useful phrases in Danish, see the inside back cover.)*

CLIMATE CHART

☐ Maximum temperature
■ Minimum temperature
– Rainfall

THE CITY'S DEVELOPMENT AND LAYOUT

Copenhagen's historic centre lies close to the Sund between Sjælland and North Amager. The present straight shorelines on both sides of the islands are of artificial origin. Over the past 700 years, millions of tree-trunks have been driven into the mud, so that castles and palaces, homes and factories could be built.

The first castle was built by Bishop Absalon of Roskilde in 1167, on the small island of Holmen just off the west bank of the Sund. Around it the settlement of Købmandshavn grew up. The

Below: Copenhagen's future
Bottom: canoeing past Slotsholm

Frederiksberg

Although Frederiksberg adjoins Vesterbro and Nørrebro, it forms a town within a town *(see pages 82–86)*. It has its own district council and its own town hall. Like many other buildings in Frederiksberg, the town hall is of a rather grand design. Frederiksberg's population, however, represents a fair cross-section of society.

Below: café life
Bottom: the quiet streets of Humleby

Holmen power base later became Slotsholmen and, on the site of the present Old Town, Købmandshavn grew into København. Until 1856 there were ramparts – now Vester Voldgade, Nørre Voldgade and Østre Voldgade – surrounding the Old Town.

To call the area within the old ramparts the Old Town is only partially true, as several large fires destroyed many original buildings and, during the 1960s and 1970s, there were some thoughtless *ad hoc* developments. Nevertheless, most museums, palaces, hotels, bars, restaurants and shopping streets are concentrated in this area. From 1968 onwards, much of the central area was converted into a traffic-free zone, and many flats and apartments have been built.

WORKING-CLASS QUARTERS

When, in the middle of the 19th century, impoverished workers poured into the already overcrowded town, it was decided to clear away the ramparts. On the other side of the old fortifications, speculators began to build mainly multi-storey tenements containing small, cramped flats. These quickly became slums. In accordance with their position beside the course of the old ramparts, the districts in this new quarter bear the names Nørrebro, Vesterbro and Østerbro.

As industry began to decline after World War II, these typically working-class quarters gradually became the catchment area for those people who couldn't afford anything better. But, given the poor state of the dwellings in each area, they cried out for redevelopment.

REDEVELOPMENT CAUSES UPROAR

Nørrebro, the oldest quarter of Copenhagen, was the first part of the city to come under the scrutiny of the town planners. Unfortunately, however, they had not devised a grand plan for the area. So the inhabitants of Nørrebro defended themselves stoutly and, during the 1960s and 1970s, the otherwise peace-loving city of Copenhagen became the scene of determined house occupations and fierce street battles.

In the end, the sceptics saw their worst fears confirmed. Initially, the newly-designed blocks looked good, but newcomers arrived and the original inhabitants were forced to move out. When redevelopment work started in Vesterbro *(see pages 28–33),* care was taken to avoid the same mistakes happening again.

The situation was rather different in Østerbro as this district wasn't as old as the other two. As well as the old working-class settlements, there are streets with spacious houses and the residents represent a wider class spectrum.

The more affluent residential areas begin north of Østerbro. Hellerup, Charlottenlund and Klampenborg are newer, compact settlements, where grand villas lie hidden behind tall hedges and gates. These quarters are part of the Gentofte and Hellerup districts, both renowned as areas for very wealthy Copenhageners. Further north lie extensive open spaces, lakes and streams.

For the inhabitants of the satellite towns to the south of the city, such leafy luxury can only be a dream. The long, coastal strip between Brøndby Strand and Køge is dominated by large residential blocks and oil tanks. Attempts are underway to make this part of greater Copenhagen a more attractive area.

Below: enjoying a beer in the sun
Bottom: city view from Vor Frelsers Kirke

THE QUEEN OF DENMARK

King Frederik IX only had daughters, so when he died in 1972, one of his brothers would have succeeded to the throne had not the constitution been changed by referendum in 1953 to enable Margrethe, the eldest daughter, to succeed in the absence of male heirs. Born on 16 April 1940, immediately after the German occupation of Denmark, Margrethe benefited from the popularity of her grandfather, Christian IX, who stayed in the country during the occupation, and was often seen out and about on the streets of Copenhagen. Margrethe II, as the intelligent and well-educated queen of a constitutional monarchy, has retained her popularity, even though she has no real power.

Below: royal photo call
Bottom: Christiania Free State graffiti

Queen Margrethe has generally refrained from commenting on matters of political sensitivity, but during the mid-1980s she could not ignore the racist attacks and the agitation against asylum seekers, which upset the generally tolerant Danes. Her statements on human rights started a nationwide debate and she was praised for her intervention. Her artistic achievements are well documented: she has designed vestments for the church, illustrated books, including J.R.R. Tolkien's *Lord of the Rings*, drawn stamps and, together with her husband, translated Simone de Beauvoir's *Tous les hommes sont mortels* into Danish.

In 1967 she married the French diplomat Henri de Laborde de Monpezat, now Prince Henrik of Denmark. He immediately won the hearts of the people when he made a speech in perfect Danish. They have two sons: Crown Prince Frederik (born 1968) and Prince Joachim (born 1969).

Prince Joachim married Princess Alexandria, the daughter of a Hong Kong business family, in 1996; however, the couple separated in 2004. Amid much publicity, Crown Prince Frederik married Crown Princess Mary, originally from Tasmania, in 2004.

THE ECONOMY

Services and administration, transport and commerce are the main sources of employment in Copenhagen. The transition from an industrialised economy to a service economy started a long time ago, and the demise of the old-style B & W dockyard has only served to underline the huge structural changes that have taken place in the city. In 1996, the last 1,200 dockworkers lost their jobs in a company that was once the biggest private employer in the city. A modern freight and container port lies to the north in Hellerup. Now only a few ferries moor in the city centre harbour. Tourism attracts about 1.8 million visitors to the city every year.

WHERE TO FIND THE CITY'S GREATS

Although it lies off the beaten track in the Nørrebro district, Assistens Kirkegård, which is both a cemetery and a park, is included in many organised tours. Because space was at a premium during the 18th century, the cemetery (1760) was laid out beyond the ramparts. Famous Danes, including Søren Kierkegaard, Christen Købke and Hans Christian Andersen, are buried here.

During the summer, the cemetery becomes a park, popular with picnickers. The main entrance is from Kapelvej (open May–Aug: 8am–8pm; Sept–Oct: 8am–6pm; bus no. 5A or 350S). Ask for a map in the Tourist Office.

Christianshavn

In Christianshavn, just across the water from the city centre, the clock seems to tick more slowly – a fact that is much appreciated by those who enjoy an alternative lifestyle in the Free State of Christiania *(see pages 79–80)*. Hardly any trace of big-city bustle remains in Christianshavn today. Where the great trading ships of old once unloaded their cargoes, pleasure boats now bob in the canals, and offices fill the massive warehouses.

a Royal Guard

HISTORICAL HIGHLIGHTS

1167 King Valdemar the Great gives Bishop Absalon of Roskilde land by the Øresund, which includes the fishing and trading settlement of Havn. Absalon builds a castle on the island of Holmen.

1254 The village of Købmandshavn or 'Merchants' Port' receives a municipal charter. The Hanseatic League, which has risen to power in the Baltic, recognises the expanding port as an important staging post for Baltic trade.

1332–40 Denmark is ruled by the counts of Holstein.

1354 Valdemar IV Atterdag unites the country and restores the throne.

1369 Absalon's castle is demolished and replaced in 1376 by København Slot.

1397 Margrethe I of Denmark forges the Kalmar Union of Denmark, Norway and Sweden under Danish leadership.

1417 Erik VII makes Copenhagen his capital and builds a palace in Helsingør.

1425 onwards Ships using the Øresund have to pay tolls. Trade flourishes and the population rises from 3,000 to 10,000.

1523–34 Kalmar Union ends with Gustav Vasa's coronation as king of Sweden. Norway remains part of Denmark.

1536 Christian III declares Protestantism to be the state religion.

1546–83 After six epidemics, sanitary conditions in the city are improved.

1588–1648 Christian IV enlarges the town and harbour and commissions the construction of many grand Renaissance-style buildings, including Rosen-

borg Slot and Børsen. Copenhagen flourishes culturally and economically. However, attempts to transform Denmark into a great European power end in disaster: during the Thirty Years' War, Sweden gains much Danish land and by 1648 Denmark is ruined.

1648–70 Reign of Frederik III who plunges the country into war with Sweden. Denmark loses a third of its land, including Skåne, to Sweden. The gates of Copenhagen and the Øresund become the border between the two countries. Fortifications are strengthened.

1665 Frederik III deprives the nobility of power and establishes an hereditary absolute monarchy.

1711 The plague claims 20,000 lives out of a Copenhagen population of 65,000.

1728 A fire destroys half of Copenhagen's housing.

1732 Christian VI replaces København Slot with the palace of Christiansborg.

1784 Land reforms under Crown Prince Frederik allow 60 percent of Danish peasants to become landowners.

1800s Overseas trade brings prosperity to the merchants, shipping companies and guilds. From 1815, many important personalities give a boost to the arts and science in Denmark's 'Golden Age'.

1801 During the Napoleonic Wars, an English fleet under Admiral Horatio Nelson succeeds in destroying much of the Danish fleet anchored in Copenhagen harbour. This forces Denmark to renounce the armed neutrality treaty of 1794, which it had entered into with Sweden, Russia and Prussia.

1807 English ships appear off Copenhagen again and demand the surrender of the Danish fleet. Much of Copenhagen is destroyed in a bombardment. The Danes join the continental alliance against England, and suffer further defeats. By 1813 the country is bankrupt.

1814 At the Treaty of Kiel, Norway is ceded to Sweden and Denmark keeps Iceland, Faroe Islands and Greenland.

1843 Tivoli Gardens open.

1847 The first railway line links Copenhagen with Roskilde.

1848–9 On 4 June 1849, Frederik VII signs a new constitution. Denmark becomes a constitutional monarchy.

1857 onwards The old ramparts are demolished to create space for dwellings. Industrialisation draws in the poor rural population. By 1900, the population of Copenhagen approaches 400,000.

1864 After the war with Prussia and Austria, Denmark cedes Schleswig, Holstein and Lauenburg to Germany.

1906 Ole Olsen founds the 'Nordisk Films Kompagni', which still exists today – the world's oldest film company.

1907 onwards With two castles destroyed by fire (1795 and 1884), work on the third Christiansborg Palace starts. In 1918, it becomes the seat of the Folketing, the Danish parliament.

1914–18 Denmark remains neutral during World War I.

1915 Women gain the right to vote.

1924 onwards Social Democrats win power. Despite the economic crisis of the 1930s a welfare state is established.

1940–5 Though wishing to remain neutral during World War II, Denmark is invaded by the German army on 9 April 1940 and used as a gate for the invasion of Norway. In return for minimal co-operation, the Danes retain limited self-government. This period of co-operation ends in 1943 when the government resigns. Denmark is recognised as one of the Allies. An underground war develops between the Danish Resistance and the Germans. Thousands of Jews escape to Sweden.

1945 Denmark is liberated by the British on 5 May.

1949 Denmark is a founder of NATO.

1950–70 Satellite towns spring up around Copenhagen. A quarter of Denmark's population lives in or near the capital.

1968 onwards Unplanned redevelopment of several older districts leads to protests by residents.

1971 Young people found the Free State of Christiania.

1972 Margrethe II succeeds to the throne. Denmark joins the EEC (today's European Union).

1993 After Denmark votes against the Maastricht Treaty in a 1992 referendum, the Danes accept a revised treaty.

2000 Øresund bridge opens between Denmark and Sweden.

2001 In a swing to the far-right, the electorate vote for Liberal Party and Danish People's Party, with their promises of stricter immigration controls.

2004 The latest royal wedding is held in Copenhagen.

2005 The Liberal Party is re-elected.

Map
on pages
20–21

Centre point

Not only is Rådhuspladsen (City Hall Square) the administrative and transport hub of Copenhagen, it is also the place from which signposts in the country measure their distance to the capital. Streets tend to have their lowest house number at the end closest to the square.

1: Around Tivoli

Rådhuspladsen (City Hall Square) – Louis Tussaud's Wax Museum – Tivolimuseet – Tivoli – Axeltorv – Tycho Brahe Planetarium

Tivoli Gardens are a symbol of typical Danish informality. Many Copenhageners have season tickets, as this pleasure park not only bustles with activity during the summer, but also serves as a meeting-place throughout the rest of the year. It has a stage for a symphony orchestra, live performances of jazz, folk and pop music take place in the pubs and cafés, and visitors will have no difficulty finding somewhere to satisfy their hunger. Twice a week from May to September, a magnificent firework display illuminates the night sky.

If Tivoli is not enough for a day out, then there are plenty of other attractions in the area, many of them within a short walk of the gardens. Start out from City Hall Square, an important Copenhagen landmark that is on nearly all the bus routes and is only a short walk from Hovedbanegården (Central Railway Station).

CITY HALL SQUARE

Preceding pages: the City of Green Spires
Below: Rådhuspladsen

Rådhuspladsen (City Hall Square) is both an institution and a source of controversy. Gatherings and demonstrations, which have moved (or

are moving or are supposed to move) the nation, take place here. Colourful neon signs and the digital news read-out provided by *Politiken*, the respected liberal newspaper, emphasise its importance as a focal point.

What causes the controversy is not its place at the heart of the nation, but the way the square has been developed. Traffic has been diverted away from the middle of the square and bus stops removed to the sides. Seating and a café lend a calmer feel to the otherwise hectic bustle. But what are those tall, dark, elongated constructions that cover the two travel and admission ticket sales points? The newspapers were full of complaints and explanations, while the architects claimed they were misunderstood.

CLASSICAL CITY HALL

The huge **Københavns Rådhus (City Hall) ❶**, which dominates the southeast side of the square, was built between 1892 and 1905 in a mix of Classical styles and northern Italian Renaissance. Bishop Absalon, the city's founder, appears on a gilded statue above the main doorway. The interior is also extravagantly finished. It may only be viewed as part of a guided tour (open Mon–Fr 3pm, Sat 10am and 11am).

In the foyer (open Mon–Fri 10am–4pm, Sat 10am–1pm) stands **Jens Olsens Verdensur**, a unique timepiece with 12 works and 19,000 parts. The world clock's mechanisms, which have to be wound up once a week, give the exact time, date, time of sunrise and sunset and other data. It's possible to climb to the balcony of the 106-metre (348-ft) tower and look down over the city centre and across the Øresund to Sweden (open 1 June–30 Sept: Mon–Fri 10am, noon and 2pm, Sat noon; otherwise Mon–Sat at noon).

Below: gilded statue of Bishop Absalon on the City Hall
Bottom: Jens Olsens Verdensur

STATUES AND FAIRYTALES

To the right of the City Hall steps, towards the busy H.C. Andersens Boulevard, it's easy to overlook the seated statue of Denmark's famous

Map
below

Danish Design Centre
Opposite Tivoli at 27–29 H.C. Andersens Boulevard, the glass-fronted Danish Design Centre (Mon–Fri 10am–5pm, Wed 10am–9pm, Sat and Sun 11am–4pm) embodies the country's preoccupation with cool, clean, elegant lines for which it has earned an international reputation. Check out the current exhibition.

fairytale writer and poet – Hans Christian Andersen really deserves somewhere better. To the left of City Hall, on Vester Voldgade, stands a pillar with a statue of two **lur players**. Erected in 1914, this model of two Bronze Age musicians is much admired. It is said – tongue in cheek – that when a virgin passes beneath the statue the players blow their horns.

BELIEVE IT OR NOT

Now on to the lighter side of this tour. One possible starting point is the American-style museum of curiosities just behind the *lur* players. **Ripley's Believe it or Not!** (mid June–Aug: 9.30am–9.30pm; Sept–mid June: 10am–6pm; Fri and Sat 10am–8pm) is based on a venerable American newspaper strip and, if you're keen to learn more about the demise of aviation pioneers, or you're interested in how you can smoke with your eyes, this attraction will be of interest to you. You can even try the chilling equilibrium tunnel.

'Lur Players' adjacent to the City Hall

WAX WORKS

Situated in a small, Renaissance villa on the other side of City Hall Square, ★ **Louis Tussaud's Wax Museum ❷** (daily 10am–6pm) may have more appeal. Personalities from the worlds of politics, history, art and show business form the basis of this skilfully staged collection of wax celebrities, which is updated from time to time. Members of the Nordic royal families are also included among the exhibits, and those who can pluck up the courage should also see the Chamber of Horrors. Louis was a descendant of Madame Marie Tussaud, whose museum in central London became the model for waxwork displays throughout the world.

A waxwork royal family

TIVOLI IN THE MAKING

Housed in the same building as the Wax Museum is the ★ **Tivolimuseet** (open May–Sept: daily 11am–6pm; otherwise Tues–Sun 10am– 4pm). In this three-storey building visitors can look behind

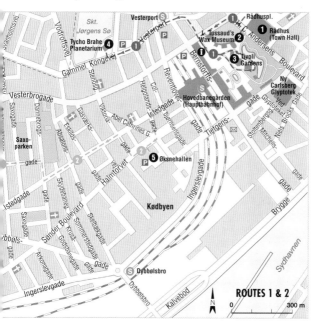

Maps
on pages
20 & 25

the scenes at the way this extraordinary pleasure park has developed. Fairground stalls, rides, games machines, flea circus, festivals, firework displays, pantomimes, variety shows, concerts, the Tivoli Guard – there are so many themes to explore, all of which arouse curiosity and a sense of anticipation, even if some of the attractions haven't stood the test of time especially well. The use of modern media, such as a short film showing pyrotechnics experts preparing the traditional firework display, helps to overcome the museum's somewhat old-fashioned appearance.

Below: Tivoli Gardens by day
Bottom: Pierrot at the
Pantomime Theatre

TIVOLI – THE FUN STARTS HERE

But even the most interesting museum is no substitute for the real thing. If you are in Tivolimuseet, you can enter the park by a special entrance. Otherwise follow H. C. Andersens Boulevard and Vesterbrogade for about 150 metres (160yd) to the **Main Entrance [A]** to ★★★**Tivoli Gardens ❸** (open mid-Apr–Sept: Sun–Thur 11am–midnight, Fri and Sat 11–1am; *see detailed map on page 25*).

Neatly uniformed attendants welcome new arrivals. These men in their old-fashioned outfits embody a sense of tradition and dignity, special qualities of Tivoli which make it more than just a pleasure park.

For proof of this, look to the left at the **Pantomime Theatre [B]**, whose actors portray characters from the Italian *commedia dell'arte*, such as Harlequin, Columbine and Pierrot. Their stories are not accompanied by tape recordings, but by a small orchestra, which then plays on between performances in the nearby **Pavilion [C]**.

SUMMER FIREWORKS

Close to Tivoli's entrance is a second, larger **open-air stage [D]**, where various performers display their talents. On Wednesday and Saturday at 11.45pm, it is also the venue for the eagerly awaited firework display. Following a tradition that goes back to the 19th century, the Tivoli

Guard also meets here. This troupe consists of about 100 boys aged between 9 and 16, who, on certain days, parade through the park in red and white uniforms and bearskin caps, playing military music. Most of these youngsters are very keen, and their enthusiasm compensates for their lack of musical experience.

A PLACE IN HISTORY

Return to the circular path through Tivoli and keep left towards H.C. Andersens Boulevard, past a small lake. At this point, it is worth investigating the park's history. The lake is the remains of a moat which surrounded the overcrowded town until 1856. The old western ramparts roughly followed the course of Vester Voldgade – hence the name – and on the present City Hall Square stood **Vesterport** (West Gate), where customs duties were levied on goods arriving in the city.

Outside the Vesterport was the cattle market and a vast wood store. It was here in the mid-19th century that the railway station was built.

With so much movement back and forth through the area, it was almost predestined to become a public park.

The driving force behind Tivoli was the polyglot entrepreneur, Georg Carstensen. He had travelled widely and seen the idea in practice in

Star Attraction
● Tivoli Gardens

Yuletide celebrations
Tivoli throws open its doors for the festive season in the run-up to Christmas each year (open mid-Nov–23 Dec: Mon–Thur 11am–10pm, Fri and Sat 11am–11pm, Sun 10am–9pm). The lake is frozen for skating and stalls dotted around the park offer tempting seasonal wares.

The fountains and open-air stage

Map on pages 20 & 25

Map on pages 20 & 25

King's edict

In the 19th century, King Christian VIII gave Tivoli's founder, Georg Carstensen, permission to create a park 'to provide the masses with suitable entertainment and fun' provided that he 'remove anything ignoble or degrading'.

Below: park patrol
Bottom: firework display

other cities. The successful formula was to be a mixture of a park, a venue for cultural events and a fair.

First, Carstensen had to persuade the king, Christian VIII, of his plan's viability, as the earmarked land followed ramparts which belonged to the army. Tivoli finally opened its gates on 15 August 1843. The first buildings were made of wood and canvas canopies so that, in the event of a military threat – the last had been in living memory between 1801 and 1814 *(see pages 14–15)* – they could be demolished quickly. One of the first attractions was a cable-car ride, a model of which can be seen in the Tivolimuseet *(see page 21)*.

Over the years, Tivoli has been modernised and greatly extended. The zigzag lines of the old ramparts have gradually disappeared and the surviving lake in the middle has become part of the park. The Chinese-style Pantomime Theatre was rebuilt in 1874 and stages pantomimes in the evening. The main entrance with its striking dome dates from 1890.

GOOD TIMES, BAD TIMES

Carstensen, who died in 1857, is remembered by a bronze statue at the entrance. In 1944, as an act of reprisal, the Germans destroyed some of

Tivoli's buildings but, within a few weeks the park was back in business, albeit on a temporary stage. Tivoli Gardens has survived a series of crises. Even when the accounts occasionally dived into the red, the attraction's future was never in serious doubt. Since 1843, some 500 million visitors have passed through the gates, and some 5 million guests now pay to enter it every year.

Tivoli pagoda

FLOODLIT WONDERLAND

With its lake and lawns, water features and flowerbeds, Tivoli fulfils its role as a traditional, landscaped garden but, as darkness falls, the atmosphere changes as thousands of electric lights come on to illuminate the scene. These, and the Chinese or Moorish-inspired buildings, create an exotic ambience, and, in keeping with the Danes' love of life, have a cheering and relaxing effect.

TIVOLI'S NIGHTLIFE

Around 30 restaurants and cafés complete the picture. Many of these offer inexpensive lunches, although in the evenings prices can be much higher. Even so, on warm summer evenings it can be difficult getting a seat in such places as Grøften or Balkonen *(see page 112)*.

These restaurants are favourite meeting places for friends, families and business people. Some of them are situated by the park's perimeter and can be reached via their own entrance, an important consideration for those establishments which have live music, as they are then accessible when Tivoli itself is closed. **Tivoli Jazzhouse** *(see page 115)* is a popular venue for jazz fans; Vise Vers Huset specialises in folk music and singalong sessions.

The main **Concert Hall [E]**, home of Sjællands Symphony Orchestra, also has a separate

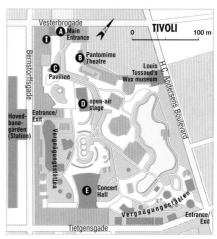

Map
on pages
20–21

entrance, so that access is possible outside the summer season. Some 100 or so concerts are held here during the season, with many free of charge.

ROLLERCOASTER RIDES

Below: a ringside seat
Bottom: Axeltorv Square

Most of the rides, fairground stalls and amusement arcades at Tivoli are concentrated along Tietgensgade. Among the most popular are the old-fashioned rollercoaster and the high-speed merry-go-rounds. Boat trips on the lake are also available. Visitors can purchase what is called a '*Tur-Pas*', a ticket which is valid for an unlimited number of rides on the day of purchase. These are sold at vending machines and ticket booths inside Tivoli.

NORTHWEST FROM TIVOLI

When you return to Tivoli's main entrance you will see **Axeltorv**, which lies on the other side of Vesterbrogade and is a square with plenty more amusement arcades. Just to the right stands **Scala**, a high-rise boutique complex *(see page 117)*. It was revamped in the late 1980s on the site of the **Scala Teater**, a theatre which came to prominence in the 1920s and '30s, when people flocked here to watch the reviews and forget their cares for a few hours. The famous chanteuse Josephine

Baker once trod the boards here in her unforget-table banana skirt. Now the Scala building only has bananas in the shop or on the menu.

The strikingly painted **Palads Teatret**, further along Axeltorv, has more than 20 screens. Unless you go for intellectual films, you will find almost everything you want playing here; lots of films for children too. You can prepare yourself for the film by stocking up at the cinema's sweet shop on the ground floor.

The final stage of the Vesterport passes first the S-station of the same name and then the **Imperial**, Copenhagen's largest cinema. The polar bear logo belongs to the Nordisk Films Kompagni *(see page 108)*.

A little further west along Gammel Kongevej lies **Skt Jørgens Lake**, one of three artificial lakes that border the western side of the city centre, offering a pleasant setting for a quiet stroll.

SEEING STARS AT THE PLANETARIUM

You simply cannot miss the ★★ **Tycho Brahe Planetarium** ❹ (open Thur–Tues 10.30am–8.30pm, Wed 9.30am–8.30pm) with its 36-metre (118-ft) high, cylindrical tower and diagonal roof. For the best view of this striking building, cross to the other side of the lake and take a walk along the promenade.

Inside the planetarium is a small exhibition on astronomy and space travel. The main draw is the film auditorium, with its 23-metre (75-ft) wide dome-shaped screen. Its *stjerneforestillinger* or 'star shows' are definitely worth sampling. Thanks to the latest computer technology, visitors can undertake a fascinating journey through space, encountering such phenomena as the Northern Lights, comets and supernovas.

The advertising for the Omnimax film performances takes up the same theme: higher, faster, wider, further. What is on offer are clips of free-climbers, rock stars and other success-ful people.

The Cassiopeia restaurant serves Danish and international cuisine (open daily 11.30am–11pm).

Star Attraction
● **Tycho Brahe Planetarium**

Tycho Brahe
Copenhagen's planetarium is named after the Danish astronomer Tycho Brahe (1546–1601). He became fascinated by astronomy after witnessing the partial solar eclipse of 1560 when he was 14. Later, Brahe's observation of a new star, called Tycho's star, made his name and he received a royal grant to set up his observatory, Uraniborg (Castle of the Heavens) on the island of Hven, in the Sound.

Below: the Tycho Brahe Planetarium
Bottom: an inside view

Map on pages 20–21

2: Vesterbro

Vesterbro – Istedgade – Øksnehallen – Saxopark – Hedebygade Kareen – Enghaven – Humleby – Carlsberg Brewery

👁 **The Railway Station**
When people arrange to meet 'under the clock', they mean the big one inside Hoved-banegården, the Central Railway Station. Built in 1912, the station has been renovated to accommodate shops, restaurants, a post office and bureau de change, all in the main hall above the platforms.

'There are more brothels, drug-addicts, gamblers and no-hopers here than anywhere else in town,' a police inspector told his colleagues in the detective film *Murder in the Dark*. On reflection, perhaps Vesterbro was lucky to have acquired this reputation, because it was spared the predatory advances of the speculators and the thoughtless building boom of the 1960s and 1970s. But the decline of this high-rise, working-class quarter, built at the turn of the century, has been arrested. By 2007, some 5 billion kroner will have been spent giving the area a facelift. This five-hour stroll through Vesterbro, possibly shortened with a bus ride or two, explores the past and witnesses some of the new developments. As you will see, this is a quarter in the midst of change.

ISTEGADE RED LIGHT DISTRICT

The route starts at the central station. Leave the station by the rear entrance, which opens out onto the red-light street, **Istedgade**, where sex is unashamedly sold to foreigners. However, the neon lights are not quite so plentiful as you might

Øksnehallen exhibition hall

expect. Shops selling everyday items, second-hand stores and pubs abound, too, and their prices are considerably lower than in the fancy shoppers' paradise by Strøget *(see page 45)*.

If you want to explore the area, then take a detour off Istedgade. Absalonsgade leads straight to Skelbækgade, where the prostitutes wait for custom during the day.

The side wall of **Halmtorvet 3** is an object lesson in the renovation business: climbers have been planted to run rampant over the trellis. Covering walls with foliage is one way of reducing noise; it also helps to protect properties from extreme temperatures and filters exhaust gases.

ØKSNEHALLEN EXHIBITION CENTRE

Beyond Halmtorvet lies an abandoned industrial area, and a new exhibition centre, ★ **Øksnehallen** ❺ (for up-to-date information on exhibitions and timings, tel: 3386 0400; e-mail: info@oeksnehallen. dk). Located in a former abattoir, Øksnehallen serves as a symbol for the re-wakening of Vesterbro. Using reclaimed building materials, the old building has been turned into an ingenious new 4,000 sq metre (43,000 sq ft) exhibition hall for the arts, business and culture, while retaining much of the character and detail of the original building. As well as temporary displays, a permanent exhibition in the building will eventually open to describe Vesterbro's revival.

SAXOPARK REVIVAL

Today it is perhaps hard to imagine that the green **Saxopark**, to the north of Istedgade on Matthæusgade, was once a row of bleak backyards and poorly-maintained multi-storey tenements. For many years that was how working people lived in large parts of Vesterbro. Up until the 1970s, Saxogade was one of the poorest districts in the city, but long before the current renovation work started, this northern section was tidied up.

Matthæusgade leads towards one of the most spectacular renovation schemes in the quarter. On

Below: Øksnehallen sculpture
Bottom: Saxopark buildings

Hedebygade: architectural detail

the right-hand side of Enghavevej lies the **Hedebygade Kareen ❻**, a restoration project from which architects, builders, town planners and environmentalists hope to learn a lot. This huge, new scheme takes into account social as well as ecological factors. It is no luxury development for well-heeled investors and tax-dodgers. All the modernisation work is benefiting the existing residents.

ECO DESIGN AT HEDEBYGADE

Features of Hedebygade Kareen scheme include planting climbers to grow up some of the exterior walls, rooftop solar panels to provide power, conduits to direct rainwater into reservoirs which will meet some of the neighbourhood's water requirements, and 'green' kitchens fitted out using environmentally-friendly materials and energy-saving equipment.

Also incorporated are 'forcing frames' attached to the facades, to serve both as a balcony and to encourage horticultural endeavour.

The highlight of the complex is probably the spacious inner courtyard that acts as a 'green lung' for the surrounding environment: it contains vegetable and herb gardens for the cooks and playgrounds for the children – anything is possible in the space.

A community hall, constructed mainly from recycled materials, sits on the sunniest spot, beneath an insulating mound of earth that forms a sun terrace in the summer and a toboggan run in the winter.

South-facing panoramic windows absorb light and heat energy, which is stored in water tanks and then fed through pipes to heat floors and even warm walls.

The work was financed by the city council and it was all finished by 2003. The main entrance to the courtyard is situated between Hedebygade 9 and 11. It has not been decided whether the courtyard will be open to the public. You may find access difficult. If so, try to find someone to help you get in.

THE ROSES OF ENGHAVEN

Enghaven Park (1928) is situated on the right of the busy Enghavevej. This is the last opportunity for a break on this tour and can be particularly rewarding if the roses are in flower. On the other side of Vesterfælledvej lies **Humleby**, truly a gem of a place. This little settlement comprises rows of houses, built between 1886 and 1891 to accommodate the Carlsberg brewery workers.

CARLSBERG BREWERY TOUR

The cobbled Ny Carlsberg Vej crosses in front of the famous ★★ **Carlsberg Brewery ❼**, which straddles the districts of Vesterbro and Valby. The brewery buildings are fascinating in themselves; a model of Thor, god of Thunder, rides his chariot on the roof. To enter the works, which employs some 1,300 people, you pass through a portal – the Elephant Gate – that is supported by four 5-metre (16-ft) high Indian elephants, carved in granite from the island of Bornholm. These sculptures, dating from 1901, are from a design by one of Copenhagen's most celebrated architects, Vilhelm Dahlerup, inspired by a similar design in the Church of Our Saviour in Copenhagen. It is no longer possible to take guided tours of the brewery itself; instead, the Visitors' Centre is open for a self-guided tour and free tastings.

Star Attraction
● **Carlsberg Brewery**

Visitors' Centre
Learn about the history of the brewing industry, taste the beers and see the dray horses in their stables at the Carlsberg Visitors' Centre, Gamle Carlsberg Vej 11 (open Tues–Sun 10am–4pm, closed public holidays and 23 Dec–1 Jan).

Below: improbably popular
Bottom: Carlsberg's elephants

Map
on pages
20–21

A TASTE OF CARLSBERG

The tour of the factory alternates between past and present. Its main sights include the historic, computer-controlled brewing hall, the modern fermenting and storage tanks, an abandoned bottling plant built at around the turn of the century, and the present-day plant, where a handful of workers keep an eye on the automated process from behind the machinery and conveyor belts. A bottle gallery displays examples of all the surviving types of Danish beer. The 20, strong Jutland horses that are lovingly cared for in the stables provide good publicity for the company. They are often seen on the city streets pulling brewery carts.

Carlsberg brewery invests heavily in advertising and, to help create a positive image, at the conclusion of the guided tour, the company lays on a generous sampling session for its guests. The beer tasting takes place in an impressive hall decorated with statues. By now it should be clear that Carlsberg is no ordinary company.

THE HISTORY OF CARLSBERG

Jacob Christian Jacobsen (1811–87) was not interested in simply taking over his father's small brewery. He had plans for a large, modern factory but, before embarking on any rash schemes, he

Above: the end product
Below: beer sampling
in progress

set about improving the basic product. In the mid-18th century Danish beer was a barely tolerable beverage, so Jacobsen toured Germany in search of the perfect brew, and he returned from Bavaria with new yeast. Jacobsen now knew he could produce something very special. By 1847, a brand new brewery on a hill *(berg)* outside the ramparts was opened. The product was to be known as Carlsberg – Carl was the name of his son. The brewery was designed by Jacob Christian Jacobsen himself (with help from the architect H.C. Stilling) in a rather austere classical style.

THE NEW BREWERY

When Carl (1842–1914) grew up he joined the family firm, but differences soon emerged between father and son. In 1881, the dispute came to a head when Carl opened the 'Ny Carlsberg' (New Carslberg) brewery right next to his father's 'Gamle Carlsberg' (Old Carlsberg). The difference in design is striking: in contrast to the classicism of the old brewery, the new buildings are elaborately decorated. The old man took his revenge by bequeathing his estate to the 'Carlsbergfond' foundation, which he had founded in 1876. This body was set up with the brewery profits to provide financial assistance to science and the arts. Carl Jacobsen also wanted to be remembered as a lover of culture and so he set up his own foundation, bequeathing his fortune to the similar 'Ny Carlsbergfond'. His first project was the construction of the 'Ny Carlsberg Glyptotek' in 1906 *(see Route 3, page 34).*

CARLSBERG TODAY

The breweries and foundations have now been merged into one company, to which the Holmegaard glass factory, the Royal Copenhagen Porcelain factory, Georg Jensen Silver and, since 1970, the Tuborg brewery also belong. Carlsberg and Tuborg beers are now brewed in 41 countries and on four continents and are drunk in more than 140 countries.

Generous patron
The Carlsberg foundation continues to support the arts and science – there is hardly a decent exhibition in the country that does not receive some money from it. Funds are administered from its headquarters in Dantes Plads opposite the Ny Carlsberg Glyptotek.

Below: the brewery facade

Map below

3: Art, Culture and Kings

Ny Carlsberg Glyptotek – Nationalmuseet – Slotsholmen – Christiansborg Palace – Royal Library and Garden – Børsen – Holmens Kirke – Thorvaldsens Museum – Holmens Kanal

Ny Carlsberg Glyptotek: the Winter Garden

This tour covers the city's main historic sights, starting with an extraordinary collection of art, funded from the sale of beer. It then goes straight to Denmark's oldest museum and on to Slotsholmen, where between the 12th and the 14th centuries Bishop Absalon's castle and the first royal palace were built. While it is true that the royal family no longer live on Slotsholmen, it remains an important centre of power, where the Folketing – the Danish parliament – still meets. It's possible to spend a day wandering around the museums, but you'll have to take a break for a snack at some time. Set out from City Hall Square in the direction of Tivoli Gardens.

NY CARLSBERG GLYPTOTEK

Take H.C. Andersens Boulevard southwards to Dantes Plads. On its west side stands a striking, classical building with a columned portal and domed

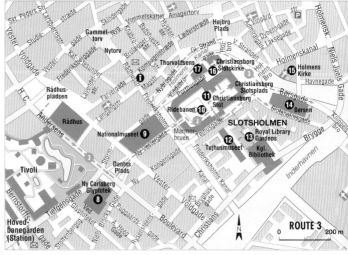

NY CARLSBERG GLYPTOTEK ◆ 35

roof, designed by the respected architect, Vilhelm Dahlerup. This is the ★★★ **Ny Carlsberg Glyptotek** ❽ (open Tues–Sun 10am–4pm; free admission on Wed and Sun) – a museum of art financed by the Carlsberg brewery *(see page 31)*. The company donates much of its profits to the arts and sciences.

CLASSICAL COLLECTION

The Glyptotek (meaning 'collection of sculpture') possesses one of northern Europe's most valuable collections and, although the emphasis is on the Egyptian, Etruscan, Greek and Roman periods, the museum's founders, Carl Jacobsen, and his wife, Ottilia, were great lovers of French art and sculpture, so there is a large French section, where works by famous artists such as Cézanne, Gauguin and Rodin are on display. New works are continually being added.

The Danish collection, which includes mainly 19th- and 20th-century works of art and sculpture, also has a solid reputation.

From an architectural point of view, the museum's highlight is the delightful Winter Garden with its fountains and abundant greenery; there is also a fine new extension by Henning Larsen, complete with glass-covered staircase.

THE NATIONALMUSEET

Opposite the main entrance to the Glyptotek, Dantes Plads narrows to become Ny Vestergade. Here, a labyrinthine building houses Denmark's largest museum, the ★★★ **Nationalmuseet** ❾ (open Tues–Sun 10am–5pm; free admission on Wed to the permanent collections). It occupies the entire block between Ny Vestergade, Stormgade, Vester Voldgade and Frederiksholms Kanal. Built in the 1740s as a palace for the crown prince, it was later extended on several occasions. From 1845, items of artistic interest from the king's treasury were stored here, and it soon developed into the highly regarded national museum.

Three of the six huge sections focus on Danish history from the Stone Age to modern times. The

Star Attractions
● **Ny Carlsberg Glyptotek**
● **Nationalmuseet**

Glyptotek's highpoints
Take a break from the treasures of Ny Carlsberg Glyptotek and treat yourself to a coffee and pastry surrounded by palm trees in the museum's indoor Winter Garden, then climb to the rooftop terrace for a bird's-eye view across the city.

Below: Degas sculpture and Cézanne paintings
Bottom: the Sun Chariot of Trundholm, Nationalmusseet

Map on page 34

Children welcome

The Nationalmuseet captures children's interests with special exhibitions (some of which are hands-on), theatrical performances and concerts.

largest section houses ethnographic exhibits from non-European countries. Of particular interest here is the Greenland exhibition with its portrayal of Inuit life. Another section focuses on the Classical era, with displays devoted to the Ancient Egyptians, the Middle East, Ancient Greece and the Roman Empire. The Royal Coin and Medal Collection has pieces from all over the world.

In addition, the Frihedsmuseet *(see page 72)*, the Open-Air Museum, which specialises in rural crafts, and the Bredemuseet, where cultural exhibitions are held (both in Lyngby) also form part of the Nationalmuseet.

PICK OF THE MUSEUM

Art made easy in the children's section

To make the most of the Nationalmuseet, ask at the reception desk for a plan of the building and then choose the sections which interest you. The atmosphere is rather austere, the attendants serious and ever-present, and visitors are expected to behave in accordance with the classical surroundings. Only the chatter of children in school parties relieves the solemn mood. If you want to take a break for refreshments, head for the museum's highly rated though pricey restaurant, or enjoy a coffee overlooking the inner court.

Ny Vestergade leads on to the Frederiksholms Kanal, where, just a few metres to the right, lies a popular *frokost* restaurant 'Kanal Cafeen' – an inexpensive alternative to the Nationalmuseet's restaurant. Culinary delights served beneath the fishing nets include *smørrebrød* with herring or eel, plaice or salmon.

EXPLORING SLOTSHOLMEN

Slotsholmen or Castle Island, the majestic centre of the city, extends to the east as far as the harbour between Sjælland and Amager, and is itself enclosed by a semi-circular canal. The first buildings here were constructed on thousands of tree trunks. Ny Vestergade opens on to the **Marmorbroen** (Marble Bridge). This rococo-style structure was built between 1741 and 1745 under the direction of Nicolai Eigtved, who was simultaneously working on the crown prince's palace. The bridge was restored in 1996, together with the two guard rooms which flank the entrance to Slotsholmen.

RIDING OUT

Behind the Marble Bridge lies the enormous, oval riding ground, the **Ridebanen** ⑩. On weekday mornings, as long as the weather is fine, there is a good chance that visitors will be able to watch the horses being put through their paces. The **Museet Kongelige Stalde og Kareter** (May–Sept: Fri–Sun 2–4pm, Oct–Apr: Sat and Sun 2–4pm), in the block to the right, accommodates the stables, royal coaches, saddles and harnesses.

THEATRICALS AT THE OLD COURT

Only a few metres away in the same block lies the court theatre, the ★ **Teatermuseet** (open Tues–Thur 11am–3pm, Sat–Sun 1–4pm). From 1767 to 1881 it was a stage for opera and drama. It is now possible for visitors to inspect the auditorium, the boxes, the stage, the changing rooms, props and other memorablia.

At the end of the riding ground, bear to the left and pass the **equestrian statue of Christian IX**

Star Attraction
● Teatermuseet

Below: Marble Bridge
Bottom: Christiansborg from the Ridebanen

Map on page 34

Below: equestrian statue of Christian IX
Bottom: Christiansborg Slot

standing in front of ★ **Christiansborg Slot ⑪**. The palace's dark granite facade, like many of the other buildings on Slotsholmen, creates a rather gloomy and melancholy impression. Small wonder then that the royal family prefers to live in Amalienborg Palace *(see page 60)*. In fact, quiet outdoor retreats on Slotsholmen are few and far between. The Danish parliament, the **Folketing**, works in the right-hand (eastern) and central (northern) blocks.

ROYAL RECEPTIONS

It is the proximity of the country's political base that requires the Queen to maintain a presence in Christiansborg. In accordance with established protocol, she invites guests to the **Royal Reception Chambers**. Meetings with foreign ambassadors take place in the Audience Room, while guests of the State dine in the Red Hall. Highly interesting are the 11 new tapestries in the Banqueting Hall by artist Bjørn Nørgard depicting 1,000 years of Danish history. The tapestries were presented to Queen Margrethe at her 50th birthday and were completed in the year 2000.

If these rooms are not in use, they are open to the public during the day. Guided tours are available in English.

PALACES OF THE PAST

Pass through the large doorway in the north wing and descend into historic Christiansborg. There were four earlier palaces, starting with the castle of Bishop Absalon, said to be the city's founder. This was extended and converted on several occasions (1137–1369). When **Slot København** (Copenhagen Castle) no longer met the requirements of the absolutist monarchs, it was demolished (1731–32). The two later palaces, which bore the Christiansborg name, both fell victim to fires (1794 and 1884).

ABSALON'S CASTLE

When in 1906 excavation work was taking place for the present palace, workmen stumbled across foundations for walls, towers, fountains and water pipes, which were part of ★ **Absalon's Castle**. These finds have been preserved in the palace cellar and can be viewed alongside photographs of the excavation work (open 1 May to 30 Sept: daily 10am–4pm; Oct–Apr: Tues–Sun 10am–4pm).

The Folketing occupies more than 320 rooms in Christiansborg. Public entry to the parliament building is not through the inner courtyard, but at the other end of the east wing. At the bottom of the staircase, a sign indicates whether and when conducted tours of the Folketing are taking place.

THE ROYAL LIBRARY

Access to the Royal Library is through a gate opposite the staircase. On the right, Tøjhusgade leads back to the Frederiksholms Kanal, which passes the Arsenal Museum, **Tøjhusmuseet** 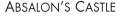 (open Tues–Sun noon–4pm). This 400-year-old, 163-metre (530-ft) long brick building houses a collection of weaponry ranging from daggers to cannons to Hawk missiles.

The **Royal Library Garden** ⑬ is Slotsholmen's 'green lung'. It is a carefully-tended area with a lawn that, unlike other parks in Copenhagen, is off limits to visitors. Near the pond, a statue recalls the philosopher Søren

Star Attractions
● Christiansborg Slot
● Absalon's Castle

Old Christiansborg
The buildings around the riding ground, including those which house the old court theatre and the stables, are the only parts of the second Christiansborg Palace, built in 1733, to have survived the fires which destroyed both that and the third palace.

Below: underground remains of Absalon's Castle
Bottom: the Arsenal Museum

Map on page 34

The Black Diamond

Love it or hate it, the Black Diamond annexe to the Royal Library is one of Copenhagen's most daring architectural projects. Designed by Århus architects Schmidt, Hammer & Lassen, the angular black polished granite facade towers over the waterside. Check the listings for special exhibitions (open Mon–Sat 10am–7pm).

Below: Royal Library garden
Bottom: the reading room

Kierkegaard. In the garden you will find the Danish Jewish Museum (open Tues–Fri 1–4pm, Sat–Sun 10am– 5pm). It is housed in an old building and has been designed by the famous architect Daniel Liebeskind who also designed the Jewish Museum in Berlin.

The Royal Library, **Det Kongelige Bibliotek** has existed since Frederik III's regency. The library is home to some 2½ million books and 55,000 manuscripts, including those written by Kierkegaard, Hans Christian Andersen and Karen Blixen. During the first half of the 16th century, the water extended right up to the present garden, and there was even a landing stage. You can see one of the mooring rings on the wall. In 1867–68 the area was filled in and by 1906 the library and garden were completed. A dramatic extension on the banks of the harbour, known as the ★ **Black Diamond**, opened in 1999 and it is now the main entrance.

A GRAND STOCK EXCHANGE

Return via the Folketing forecourt and then take two right turns. In front stands what is probably the most impressive edifice on Slotsholmen, the ★ **Børsen** ⓮ (Stock Exchange). Today, it can only be viewed from outside. Originally it was a warehouse in Dutch Renaissance style, dating from the early 17th century.

For King Christian IV, a great lover of pomp and splendour, the elongated, two-storey building was not grand enough, so in 1625 he commissioned the first of 18 striking gables and the 54-metre (177-ft) high spire – the latter is made up of four entwined dragons' tails. The three golden crowns on top represent Denmark, Norway and Sweden. In the middle of the 19th century, the currency and security dealers moved into the building, hence its name. Although these traders have since found a new home, the interior is still used as offices. The ornamentation and sculptures on the exterior reveal that it is some time since the building was last restored.

THE MARINERS' CHURCH

On the other side of the street and **Holmens Kanal**, the tower of ★ **Holmens Kirke**  (open 15 May–15 Sept: Mon–Sat 9am–2pm; otherwise Mon–Sat 9am–noon) points skyward. The church was built originally as a smithy for making anchors, but in 1619, on the orders of Christian IV, it was turned into a church for mariners' families. Two of Denmark's maritime heroes, Niels Juel (1629–97) and Peter Tordenskjold (1690–1720), who both achieved several victories over the Swedish fleet, are buried here, but ordinary seamen who lost their lives in the two world wars are also remembered. Because of its isolated position, Holmens Kirke survived earlier fires and has retained its original baroque pulpit and altar, an unusual achievement for a Copenhagen church. One particularly interesting piece is the 1-metre (3-ft) high font, dating from 1646, which bears the initials of Christian IV. It is said that it was used to baptise African slaves.

THE PALACE CHAPEL

Slotsholmen has its own church. To get there, cross to the northwest corner of **Christiansborg Palace Square**, with its equestrian statue of Frederik VII. The inscription translates as 'The love of the people is my strength.'

Star Attractions
● **View of the Børsen**
● **The Black Diamond**

Below: view of the Børsen
Bottom: the Black Diamond
extension to the Royal Library

Map on page 34

Below: Ganymede statue, Thorvaldsens Museum
Bottom: rowing on Holmens Kanal

Christiansborg Slotskirke ⑯ stands at the point where the river bends sharply. It dates from 1826 and managed to withstand the destructive fire of 1884, but not an emergency flare that went off course in 1992. The roofing timbers caught fire and the copper dome collapsed. Fortunately, most of the precious fittings were saved and the church was restored to its former splendour.

THORVALDSENS MUSEUM

Cross **Prins Jørgens Gård** to ★**Thorvaldsens Museum** ⑰ (open Tues–Sun 10am–5pm). Berte. Thorvaldsen *(see page 103)* is regarded as one of Denmark's greatest classical sculptors.

In 1781, at the tender age of 11, the young Bertel was accepted by the Copenhagen Art Academy. Later he won a scholarship to Rome. where he lived for more than 40 years. He received commissions from the Vatican and many European kings and princes, who appreciated the aesthetic ideals of antiquity.

Thorvaldsen returned to Copenhagen in 1838 and was appointed an honorary citizen. On his death six years later, he bequeathed his works, his own collection and his estate to the nation on the condition that a museum was built for the artistic treasures. His plans, castings, originals and replicas, plus his antiques – including examples

of Egyptian, Greek, Etruscan and Roman works – and his collection of paintings, are all on display here. It's worth taking a stroll around the outside of the museum to admire the life-size frieze, which was designed under the supervision of the respected architect M.G. Bindebøll. It shows Thorvaldsen's triumphant return to Copenhagen and the arrival of his sculptures at the museum. The master himself is buried in the museum's inner courtyard.

ART AND ANTIQUES ON NYBROGADE

Both the Slotskirke and Thorvaldsens Museum are situated by Vindebrogade and the **Holmens Canal**. If you cross to the other side of the canal and walk east along Nybrogade, you will pass a row of art galleries, antique shops and restaurants. The brick building on the corner of Nybrogade and Naboløs is the Ministry of Culture.

CRUISE FROM GAMMEL STRAND

Nybrogade becomes **Gammel Strand** ('Old Beach'). This refers to the time before any houses or palaces were built on Slotsholmen, and the waters of the Øresund extended this far up.

Until the 1950s, it was the site of the fish market. Only one or two of the market stalls remain, catering primarily for the tourist trade. A statue on the **Højbro** bridge recalls the colourful 'fishwives' who were once key figures in the everyday life of the district.

One part of Copenhagen life that has survived is the famous 'Krogs Fiskerestaurant' *(see page 112)*. Enjoy one of its fine – if expensive – fish dishes, after an exhilarating cruise in one of the sightseeing boats which leave from Gammel Strand.

The redesigned, traffic-calmed **Højbro Plads**, at the northern end of Gammel Strand, is the setting for a modest market. Bishop Absalon, the city's founder, surveys the Højbro from his horse. After the relative calm of Slotsholmen, the buzzing hive of activity in the commercial heart of the city comes as quite a shock to the system.

Star Attraction
● **Thorvaldsens Museum**

👁 **Harbour bus**
Give your feet a rest with a trip on the harbour bus, which stops along the waterfront between the Royal Library's Black Diamond building and Knippelsbro, Nyhavn, Holmen and Nordre Toldbod, south of the Little Mermaid.

Højbro Plads

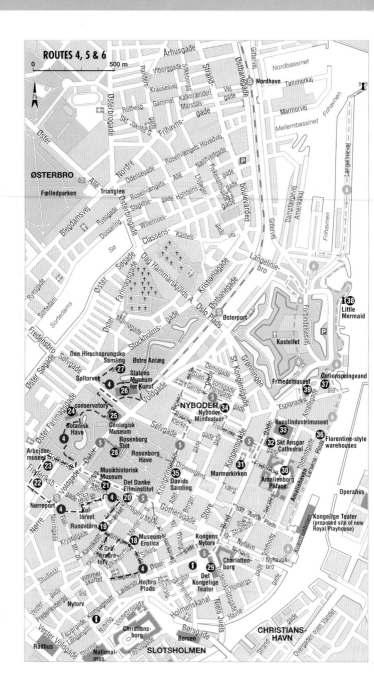

ROUTES 4, 5 & 6

0   500 m

4: Shops and Museums

Amagertorv – Museum Erotica – Gråbrødretorv – Skindergade – Rundetårn – Filmhuset – Arbejdermuseet – Botanisk Have – Geologisk Museum – Statens Museum for Kunst

Map opposite

In many circles, the mere mention of the word 'erotic' is greeted with a stony silence. Some may regard erotic films as good entertainment, but few would class them as art and even fewer would be interested in the history of the genre. Attitudes are different in Copenhagen, where there's even a museum devoted to the genre.

Start this tour at Amagertorv. Take a stroll past the tempting shops in Strøget and end with a wander through the parks and gardens to the north of the city centre.

WINDOW SHOPPING ON AMAGERTORV

Amagertorv, just north of Gammel Strand, was an important marketplace in the city's early days. Now, it is just a small part of the busy 1.6-km (1-mile) long pedestrianised **Strøget**, Denmark's top shopping street. Amid the hustle and bustle of shoppers, it is easy to overlook the delightful **Storkespringvandet** (Stork Fountain, 1894). If you look closely, you will see that the three birds resemble herons rather than storks. From an architectural point of view, the centrepiece of the square is the Dutch Renaissance-style No. 6, which dates from 1616 and so ranks as one of the city's oldest buildings. It is now used by one of Denmark's most prestigious companies, Royal Copenhagen, as a showroom for its chinaware, and is flanked by two illustrious neighbours: the silversmith Georg Jensen to the right and the modern design store Illums Bolighus to the left.

ROYAL COPENHAGEN PORCELAIN

As you would imagine, **Royal Copenhagen** has something to do with the Danish monarchy. When the porcelain factory was founded in 1775, the

Shopping on Strøget
The 1.6-km (1-mile) long pedestrian mall known as Strøget winds through the heart of Copenhagen's shopping district. Starting at Rådhuspladsen, Strøget incorporates five streets and four squares before opening out on to Kongens Nytorv. All the big names in shopping are represented, while buskers and street vendors add to the atmosphere. Explore the quieter streets to left and right for interesting bars, cafés and smaller, more exclusive shops.

Royal Copenhagen Porcelain

Map on page 44

Eating out at Illums

The top floor of that centre of modern design, Illums Bolighus, in Amagertorv, is the perfect place for rest and refreshment, with a choice of café or restaurants.

royal family were majority shareholders. Later on, they took it over completely, but now Royal Copenhagen is an independent company and part of the Carlsberg empire. The city centre **showroom** in Amagertorv (open Mon–Fri 10am–7pm, Sat 10am–5pm; June–Sept: Sun only noon–5pm) sells complete sets of china and individual pieces, including the 'Blue Fluted' and 'Flora Danica' designs – all hand-painted, some requiring thousands of brushstrokes. Although the porcelain is usually of a traditional design, the glassware comes in modern shapes and colours, both as ornamental pieces and functional objects. The Factory Shop *(see Route 8, page 86)* offers some good value seconds.

GEORG JENSEN SILVERWARE

The silverware shop, **Georg Jensen** (No.4; opening times as for Royal Copenhagen, above), exemplifies fine craftmanship. Since it was founded in 1904, the company has had two specialisms: cutlery and tableware, and jewellery. Georg Jensen was both a trained silversmith and a sculptor. When he died in 1935, the *New York Times* described him as one of the finest silver designers of the past 300 years.

Part of his company's reputation is derived from his reliance on contemporary artists. These craftsmen were skilled in manipulating not just silver, but other materials such as steel – and this proved useful during the years when the price of silver was prohibitive. The finest of Jensen's products can be admired in the showroom and the adjoining **Georg Jensen Museum**.

Georg Jensen for silverware

MODERN DESIGN AT ILLUMS BOLIGHUS

Illums Bolighus (No. 10; opening times as for Royal Copenhagen, above) contains countless examples of excellent contemporary Danish design, from beds to bottle openers, although potential buyers will need to go armed with a bulging wallet. A wander through the open galleries is definitely worthwhile, even if only to ook. You'll find smaller, more affordable items on the ground floor.

Købmagergade is another busy, traffic-free shopping street. It is worth knowing where the post office is (No. 33) but otherwise, there are few buildings of interest. The restaurant Hovedvagten above the post office offers good food and a great view.

MUSEUM EROTICA REVEALS ALL

Copenhagen, with its liberally-minded populace, is one of the few places in Europe that would tolerate a ★**Museum Erotica** (open May–Sept: daily 10am–11pm; Oct–Apr: Sun–Thur 11am–8pm, Fri–Sat 10am–10pm). Located at 24 Købermagergade, the museum is not simply a display of naked bodies. The management has sought to discriminate between love, sex and commercial pornography. So, as long as the word 'sex' doesn't cause undue embarrassment, you'll probably enjoy seeing how eroticism and sexuality have been expressed since the time of the ancient Greeks.

The further you ascend the more explicit the exhibits become. When you reach the fourth floor, a dozen videos are showing erotic films, from 1920s black and white to todays full-blown colour.

Star Attraction
● **Museum Erotica**

Below: shoppers on Amagertorv
Bottom: Illums Bolighus lighting

Map on page 44

However, not every visitor responds equally to the bare facts as displayed here, and some unsuspecting tourists have been known to beat a hasty retreat when they realise what they have let themselves in for.

STREETLIFE ON GRÅBRØDRETORV

Below: refreshment on Grabrødretorv
Bottom: exquisite glass

A shortcut through Løvstræde leads to **Gråbrødretorv**. This delightful cobbled square with a huge plane tree has been spared from traffic for many years, and that partly explains the reason for its numerous pubs and restaurants. When the sun shines, customers quickly spill out onto the pavement.

Gråbrødretorv owes its name, the 'market of the Grey Brothers', to the Franciscan monastic order. The monks, known locally as the 'Grey Brothers', had a monastery here from 1238 to 1530. All the nearby buildings were destroyed in the Great Fire of 1728 apart from the vaults of the abandoned monastery.

Today, the 'Peder Oxe', a favourite restaurant with Copenhageners *(see page 112)*, occupies the site above the cellar (No. 11). The compact row of houses (Nos. 1–11) is typical of the buildings that appeared after the Great Fire – solid walls instead of half-timber, three to four floors, a mansard roof projecting as a gable.

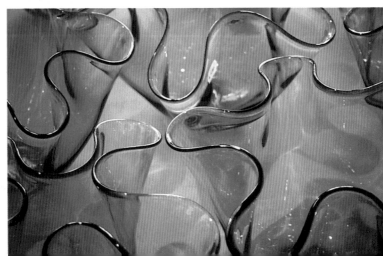

A fountain in the square was donated to the city when it celebrated its 800th birthday in 1967.

ANTIQUES-HUNTING IN FIOLSTRÆDE

If you like shopping you can take a short detour to **Fiolstræde**, west of the square. There are a number of interesting antiquarian bookshops. Towards the northwest, Gråbrødretorv opens on to **Skindergade**, which then leads back to Købmagergade. One of the oldest streets in Copenhagen, Skindergade housed the town's skin and fur traders.

Some of the fine **half-timbered houses** in Skindergade have survived both fires and property speculators. Number 11 in red and – if you go through the gate – the pretty yellow house in the rear courtyard at No. 8, both date from the first half of the 18th century.

THE ROUND TOWER

Back in Købmagergade, you will find yourself at the foot of the ★ **Rundetårn** ⑲ (open June–Aug: Mon–Sat 10am–8pm, Sun noon–8pm; Sept–May: Mon–Sat 10am–5pm, Sun noon–5pm). Christian IV had the Round Tower built in 1642 as an observatory. Royalty, such as Tsar Peter the Great, and other dignitaries reached the top by means of a spiral walkway 209 metres (685 ft) long and wide enough to accommodate a carriage. The fine view from the 36-metre (118-ft) tower takes in the whole of Copenhagen. The observatory is open in winter (Oct–Mar: Tues and Wed 7–10pm). On the premises is a Bibliotekssalen (Library Hall), offering changing exhibits on culture, art, history and science.

DENMARK'S FILM HERITAGE

It is only a few metres across Landemærket to **Det Danske Filminstitut** ⑳, home of **Cinemateket** (performances: Tues–Fri 10am–10pm, Sat–Sun noon–10pm, closed Mon). Not many people are aware that, in the years before World War I,

Star Attraction
● Rundetårn (Round Tower)

Latin Quarter
The area centred on Gråbrødretorv is home to Copenhagen's cathedral and university. Our Lady's Church, the neoclassical cathedral on Nørregade, designed in 1829 by C.F. Hansen, contains statues by the sculptor Bertel Thorvaldsen. Also on Nørregade is the main building of the University of Copenhagen, founded in 1479.

The Rundetårn

Record breakers
Experience some record-breaking endeavours at the **Guinness World of Records Museum**, 16 Østergade (open daily 10am–6pm), near Kongens Nytorv. Discover how 1.3 million dominoes tumble and what it feels like to drive at 500km/h (300mph).

Denmark was one of the world's leading cinematographic nations *(see page 108)*, so it is all the more interesting to delve into the history of Danish films via the performances that take place here (many of them with English subtitles).

Opposite the film institute, on the corner of Gothersgade (No. 87), stands 'Kongens Kælder', a *frokost* restaurant. You may be tempted by a delicious *smørrebrød*, but it is open only on weekdays from 11am–4pm *(see page 113)*.

MUSICAL NOTES ON ÅBENRÅ

From the cinema to music. Situated in narrow Åbenrå, the **Musikhistorisk Museum ㉑** (open May–Sept: daily 1–3.50pm, closed Thurs; Oct–April: Mon, Wed, Sat, Sun 1–3.50pm) is a source of fascination to anyone who loves music. In particular, its collection of instruments from the past 1,000 years steal the show.

Occasionally, the History of Music Museum stages classical concerts, often using some of the ancient instruments normally kept for display. Ask at the entrance for details of any forthcoming events.

Hausergade connects Åbenrå with the traffic-calmed **Kultorvet**, a popular meeting-place for young people. The Café Klaptræet *(see page 113)* is symbolic of the crisis that beset the Danish film industry earlier in the last century, when it had to contend first with the confusion of World War I, and later with the emigration of film stars to America. Originally a café and cinema, only the furniture, posters and film rolls recall the glory days of the former cinema round the corner.

CARICATURIST MAKES HIS MARK

It's worth making a brief stop outside No. 9 in **Rosengården** to admire the small plaque. This portrayal of the Danish philosopher Søren Kierkegaard was the work of the caricaturist, Christian Klæstrup (1820–82), who once lived in this building. He was Denmark's first cartoon-

Fiddler on the loose

ist, and he had to contend with the humourless censors who viewed all his drawings as an attack on the authorities.

JEWISH MEMORIAL ON ISRAEL PLADS

Follow **Fiolstræde**, Copenhagen's third shopping street, for a short distance to the underground S-station of Nørreport on the main Nørre Voldgade. There is an early 20th century **telephone kiosk** at the junction which, until recently, was used as a box office for concert tickets.

On the other side of Nørre Voldgade, which follows the course of the old ramparts, Vendersgade cuts through to **Israel Plads ㉒** and Rømersgade. This square was so named in 1968 to recall the 25th anniversary of the German persecution of Danish Jews during World War II. The red stone beside Rømersgade was presented by the Israeli government in 1975.

MARKET PLACE

From Monday to Saturday, fruit and vegetable stalls occupy the northern side of Israel Plads along Frederiksborggade. On Saturday during the summer months, the produce sellers are joined by a lively flea market. What is offered for sale here, however, would probably be best described as

Below: a young visitor at Israel Plads
Bottom: enjoying a drink outside

Map on page 44

bric-a-brac rather than antiques *(see page 117)*. Not usually any bargains, but can be fun.

The Workers' Museum

Historical museums usually focus on the great and the good. ★★ **Arbejdermuseet** ㉓ (The Workers' Museum), 22 Rømersgade (open daily 10am–4pm) tells a different story, and in a livelier and more informative way than is normal. Many socialist heroes, such as Wilhelm Liebknecht, August Bebel, Rosa Luxembourg and Clara Zetkin, spoke at public meetings in the large room at the back of this building. It was, therefore, the ideal place for a museum dedicated to the class struggle.

Below and bottom: inside the Arbejdermuseet

The exhibitions begin in 1870 at a time when many employees were being exploited by industrialisation, when workers' leaders found themselves in prison and the police spied on meetings. Life was harsh and conditions in the factories bleak. One of the most impressive displays traces the Sørensen family through three generations, mainly in the years before World War II. It shows how impoverished farmers arrived in the towns full of hope, how the world economic crisis affected everyday life, how working conditions changed in the various professions, and the improvements that had to be fought for.

TRADITIONAL EATS

The 1950s in Denmark were characterised by an improving social security safety net and greater purchasing power, but men and women still did not receive equal pay and there was a shortage of decent homes. It was during this period that canteens opened to provide cheap cakes and drinks for working people. The Café & Ølhalle 1892 *(see page 113)* situated in the Arbejdermuseet serves traditional Danish fare.

A WALK IN THE BOTANICAL GARDENS

Israel Plads and Rømersgade have developed on the site of the old ramparts, as have the green areas to the north and south.

The ★ **Botanisk Have** (Botanical Gardens), just to the north of Gothersgade, is a delightful environment for a relaxing stroll (gardens: open May–Sept: daily 8.30am–6pm; Oct–Apr: Tues–Sun 8.30am–4pm; conservatory: daily 10am–3pm; other greenhouses: Wed, Sat and Sun 1–3pm). Some 10 hectares (25 acres) of land contain a variety of plant life, including herbs, shrubs and rock gardens. Many of the plants are native to northern Europe, but some are exotic and come from further afield.

The impressive **conservatory** ㉔, opened in 1874 with the rest of the Botanisk Have, contains a marvellous collection of tropical and sub-tropical flora. There is a café just behind the conservatory, which serves refreshments during the summer. The benches around the ponds are always very popular, but the Botanical Gardens cannot really compete with Rosenborg Have or Frederiksberg Have, as here the public are obliged to keep off the lawns. The small **Botanisk Museum** is only opened for special exhibitions.

THE GEOLOGY MUSEUM

A Renaissance building in the Botanical Gardens houses the **Geologisk Museum** ㉕ (Tues–Sun 1–4pm), a treasure trove of curiosities,

Below: Café & Ølhalle
Bottom: the Botanical Gardens

Map
on page
44

👁 **Cultural benefactors**
It is interesting to ponder that a large part of Denmark's cultural heritage is accessible to the nation thanks to the benevolence of two individuals: one who made his fortune out of tobacco, Heinrich Hirschsprung (Den Hirschsprungske Samling, *this page*), and the other who made it out of beer, Carl Jacobsen (Ny Carlsberg Glyptotek, *page 34*).

Below: Statens Museum for Kunst interior
Bottom: an exterior view

which will be of interest to the layperson. The meticulously arranged mineral collection, the meteorites and the Greenland exhibition are the main focal points. The entrance to the museum is on Øster Voldgade 5–7 (it is not possible to enter the museum directly from the Botanical Gardens).

Fɪɴᴇ Aʀᴛ ɪɴ Øꜱᴛʀᴇ Aɴʟᴀ̊ɢ

To the north of the wide Sølvgade, the green belt continues with the Østre Anlæg. This quiet, unassuming park provides the right setting for two art museums.

One grand building dating from 1896 houses the extremely worthwhile National Gallery, the ★★ **Statens Museum for Kunst** ㉖ (open Tues– Sun 10am–5pm, Wed until 8pm). Any resemblance to the Ny Carlsberg Glyptotek is not a coincidence – the design for both originates from the same drawing board, that of Vilhelm Dahlerup.

Inside, the fine collection of European art dates from around 1530. The main themes are Danish painting and French 19th-century painting. A gleaming new four-storey building extending towards the park has been built to house the gallery's collection of modern art. Exhibitions are held here, too.

A collection of copperplate engravings and drawings, as well as montages by children, are also of particular interest.

Tʜᴇ Hɪʀꜱᴄʜꜱᴘʀᴜɴɢꜱᴋᴇ Cᴏʟʟᴇᴄᴛɪᴏɴ

The second temple of culture in Østre Anlæg is **Den Hirschsprungske Samling** ㉗ (open Wed– Mon 11am–4pm). The gallery focuses on Danish art with a preference for 19th-century and early 20th-century painting, including works by the Skagen painters such as Michael and Anna Ancher and P.S. Krøyer. The collection owes its survival to the tobacco magnate, Heinrich Hirschsprung (1836–1908), who donated it to the state in 1902.

5: Route of the Royal Life Guard

Rosenborg Slot – Rosenborg Have – Kongens Nytorv – Frederiksstaden – Amalienborg Palace – Marmorkirken – Skt Ansgars Kirke – Kunstindustrimuseet – Nyboder – Davids Samling

Map on page 44

Every day at 11.30am, the Royal Life Guard marches from its base near Rosenborg Castle through the city centre to arrive at Amalienborg Palace, for the changing of the guard ceremony exactly half-an-hour later. If the queen is in residence, the grand ceremony is carried out to musical accompaniment. While the soldiers with their thick bearskins may not be allowed to break their journey for a delicious snack, or stand and stare admiringly at historic buildings, you can. To the north-west of Amalienborg lies the modest, but attractive Nyboder residential area.

Allow about four to five hours for this tour. To reach the starting point at Rosenborg Castle, you will need to take the S-train to Nørreport or bus numbers 14, 42 or 43.

ROSENBORG SLOT

Christian IV (1577–1648) loved grand festivals and splendour, so the medieval, rather gloomy Copenhagen Castle had little appeal for him. He ran the affairs of state from Frederiksborg Slot,

Below: Rosenborg Slot
Bottom: the Royal Life Guard

Map on page 44

some 35 km (22 miles) to the north-west of Copenhagen *(see page 98)*, but he really wanted a suitable residence in Copenhagen, so in 1605 he ordered work to start on a palace just outside the city walls. It was 1624, after several alterations and enlargements, before Christian declared himself content with the outcome: ★★★ **Rosenborg Slot** ㉘ (June–Aug: daily 10am–5pm; May and Sept: daily 10am– 4pm; Oct: daily 11am–3pm; Nov–April: 11am–2pm, closed Mon). Christian had commissioned highly-regarded architects from the Netherlands, and their work was a masterpiece of Dutch Renaissance. Constructed from red bricks, the facade was decorated with light sandstone. It was secured by a moat with drawbridge and surrounded by a magnificent rose garden, hence the name.

Below: the Crown Jewels
Bottom: a palace full of treasures

NO KING FOR THE CASTLE

No monarch ever resided permanently at Rosenborg. In 1722, less than 100 years after the castle was built, it was replaced as second residence by Fredensborg Slot, near the delightful lake known as Esrum Sø in northern Sjælland.

Rosenborg was more or less abandoned to become the 'royal family's store-room'. All the state treasures were brought here, as there was either no use or no space for them in the inhabited

residences. Consequently, the rooms in Rosenborg were splendidly furnished. They were opened up to the public in 1838, and attract thousands of visitors every year. It is certainly worth obtaining the guidebook, which lists all the relics on display in the Marble Apartment, Glass Chamber, Knights' Hall and the Bronze Chamber. Finally, the Danish Crown Jewels wait patiently behind glass for their next outing. The restaurant Trakførstedet just outside the castle is well worth visiting for a break or lunch.

A STROLL IN THE KING'S GARDEN

★★ Rosenborg Have lies beside Gothersgade. This park, sometimes known as **Kongens Have** (or King's Garden) was laid out when Rosenborg Slot was built. Converted into an English-style garden in 1820, with its tall, old trees, statues, grassy lawns and shady walks, it is now an important breathing space in the densely populated city.

On a fine day, children from nearby nursery schools scramble on the playgrounds, weary legs rest on the park benches and tired minds enjoy a nap on the grass, but the Royal Life Guard, whose job it is to patrol the castle and protect the Crown Jewels, keeps an eye on passers-by.

MARCHING WITH THE GUARDS

The barracks of the Royal Life Guard are situated next to the castle. Every morning, the changing of the guard is rehearsed on the exercise ground beside the barracks. Those sightseers who wish to accompany the guards as they make their way through the city start to congregate outside the gates at around 11am.

As the troops emerge in formation, a frantic scene ensues as tourists, often not too sure of the route the soldiers will take, hurry ahead with their cameras and videos in the hope of a good shot. The troops march past them and the whole episode starts again.

Although they disregard the antics of the eager tourists, the guardsmen are not exempt from the

Star Attractions
● Rosenborg Slot
● Rosenborg Have

Life Guard Museum
The history of the Royal Life Guard since its foundation in 1658 is documented in the Livsgardens Historiske Samling (open May–Sept: Tues and Sun 11am–3pm; Oct–April: Sun 11am–3pm) next to Rosenborg Slot.

Below: the Life Guard barracks
Bottom: the Danish flag

Map on page 44

routines of city life – they have to stop at red traffic lights. If the queen is in residence, then the soldiers and band take the long route via Gothersgade, Nørre Voldgade, Frederiksborggade, Købmagergade, Østergade, Kongens Nytorv, Bredgade, Sankt Annæ Plads and Amaliegade. Otherwise, the shorter tour without musical accompaniment follows Gothersgade, Christian IX's Gade, Gammel Mønt, Kr. Bernikows Gade and Østergade to Kongens Nytorv.

AROUND KONGENS NYTORV

Follow **Østergade** at the northern end of Strøget for a short distance. The **Pistolstræde** passage on the left-hand side leads off on a short detour to cafés, restaurants and shops, where prices are comparable with those on Strøget.

Bang & Olufsen showroom

Strøget and Østergade emerge onto a huge and historic square: **Kongens Nytorv**. Its origins date from the end of the 17th century, when Christian IV was looking to expand the city northwards. His grandson, Christian V, had something grander in mind, namely a large, central square surrounded by stately buildings, which would fulfil Denmark's absolutist rulers' desire for splendour and panache. In No. 26 stands the **Bang & Olufsen** showroom. Step inside for the ultimate in hi-fi design.

ARCHITECTURAL HIGHLIGHTS

The oldest surviving building, **Charlottenborg Slot** (1672–83; *see page 67*) looks out towards the Nyhavn harbour. Others have been altered or replaced by more modern edifices, such as the Royal Theatre, **Det Kongelige Teater ㉙**, a neo-Renaissance building dating from 1874. Two of Denmark's most celebrated writers, Adam Oehlenschlæger and Ludvig Holberg, stand by the steps to welcome arrivals. Two more fine facades flank the start of Strøget: on the left is the department store **Magasin du Nord** (1894; *see page 117*), on the right the **Hotel d'Angleterre** (1874; *see page 124*), Denmark's top hotel.

The square has just been redesigned to give it its grandeur back and reduce traffic. New trees have been planted and new pavement laid. The equestrian statue shows Christian V. Cast in lead in 1688, the monarch's weight caused irreparable damage to the horse, so in 1946 a new bronze statue was made to replace the original.

GOLD OF THE NORTH

At the point where Bredgade joins Kongens Nytorv, the **Ravhuset** studio and shop (open May–Sept: 10am–8pm; Oct–April: 10am–6pm) tempts tourists with its large collection of amber. Retrieving and processing amber washed up on the beach is a traditional industry in Jutland, and the translucent fossil resin has become a popular Danish jewellery item.

STATELY FREDERIKSSTADEN

Bredgade marks the gateway to **Frederiksstaden**, probably the most ambitious building project since the Middle Ages. In 1749, to the northeast of Kongens Nytorv, a district emerged where the nobility and the well-to-do middle classes could distance themselves from the rest of the city's residents. Their stately homes lined streets laid out in a regular pattern, in contrast to the winding

Below: statue of Christian V
Bottom: the Royal Theatre

Map on page 44

streets of medieval Copenhagen. Court architect, Nicolai Eigtved was responsible for the ground-plan, of which Bredgade forms a part. The city's establishment has retained its preference for this quarter. Advertising agencies, solicitors and other offices vie for an address in **Palægade** and **Sankt Annæ Passage** (between Bredgade and Store Kongensgade), while the district's cafés, restaurants and boutiques compete equally strenuously for these wealthy professionals' custom.

FOOD FOR THOUGHT

Below: evening view of Amalienborg
Bottom: the Amalienborg Palace facade

The short route of the Royal Life Guard follows Bredgade as far as Frederiksgade; the longer march crosses **Sankt Annæ Plads** and then bears left into **Amaliegade**. A major attraction of this quiet street, with its classical and baroque facades, is the tastefully decorated 'Amalie' *frokost* restaurant at Amaliegade 11 (open Mon–Sat 11.30am–5pm).

AMALIENBORG PALACE

Just beyond the colonnade, the guardsmen reach their destination: ★★ **Amalienborg Palace** ❸⓪. The octagonal square, overlooked by four ornate rococo palaces – initially occupied by four aristocratic families – was always intended to be the

centrepiece of Frederiksstaden. When the second Christiansborg Palace burnt down in 1794, Christian VII moved his residence to Amalienborg. The colonnade was to link Christian VII's palace (to the right of the palace square) with that of the Crown Prince (on the left), where Margarethe II now lives. Traditionally, the royal family's rooms have been shared out among several palaces.

CHANGING OF THE GUARD

If visiting Amalienborg Palace, try to time it to include the daily ★★ **Changing of the Guard** at noon. If the flag is flying, then the queen is in residence and the full Changing of the Guard ceremony will take place. Precise footsteps, manoeuvres and spoken commands ensure that the event goes off smoothly.

When the officer in charge of the new company has received the order from his predecessor, ten soldiers replace their counterparts at the palace entrances, while the rest disappear through a gate into the interior of the castle. Every two hours, the guards change duties. Finally, the original contingent set off back to their barracks along Frederiksgade, Store Kongensgade and Gothersgade.

Spectators may only take photographs of the ceremony from specified places, although after the official handover there is little to see. In any case, attendants are on hand to ensure that the rules are followed. People whose behaviour is deemed to be too casual, perhaps if they sit down on the pavement or steps, will be approached and reprimanded.

ONWARDS TO THE MARBLE CHURCH

The area around the equestrian statue in the centre of the square is normally out of bounds. Sitting astride the horse is the man who lent his name to Frederiksstaden, Frederik V. The sculptor, J.F. Saly, took 20 years to complete the statue. It was renovated in 1998. If you are standing in the middle of the palace square and

Star Attractions
● Amalienborg Palace
● Changing of the Guard

Palace Museum
Housed in the northern building of Amalienborg Palace is the small Palace Museum of Christian VIII (open May–Oct: daily 10am–4pm; Nov–April: Tues–Sun 11am–4pm), which contains the private chambers of kings Christian IX (1863–1906), Frederik VIII (1906–12), Christian X (1912–47) and Frederik IX (1947–72).

Statue of Frederick V, Amalienborg

Map on page 44

The Marble Church

cannot decide which road you should take, you will almost certainly be drawn by the huge, copper dome of the ★ **Marmorkirken** ㉛ (open Mon–Thurs 10am–5pm; Fri–Sun noon–5pm. Dome: open mid-June– Aug: daily 1pm and 3pm; Sept–June: Sat–Sun 1pm and 3pm).

The church's proper name is **Frederiks Kirke**. Frederik V had in mind a splendid rococo church for Frederiksstaden, and in 1749 imported vast quantities of marble from Norway. But even a royal contractor can run out of money, and work slowed down. In 1770, just four years after the king's death, the project was cancelled.

MODELLED ON ST PETER'S IN ROME

The partially completed building was left to decay for more than 100 years, but in 1874 the industrialist Tietgen financed the completion of the project. He retained the completed marble base and put most of his money into other extravagant features. Above the portal, 16 zinc statues represent important personalities in Danish church history, while the Italian baroque dome is modelled on St Peter's in Rome. The dome, which can be viewed close-up from a gallery, dominates the interior, too. Particularly striking features include the royal box and the paintings, which depict the 12 apostles.

THE CHURCHES OF BREDGADE

If you are in the mood for admiring churches, then a short distance northeast from the Marble Church, on the same side of Bredgade, stands the Russian Orthodox **Alexander Newsky Kirke** (1883). The interior, however, is closed to the public.

The doors to the Catholic cathedral of **Skt Ansgars Kirke** ㉜ are usually open on four days (Tues–Fri 10am–4pm). This church suffered a similar fate to that of the Marble Church. The Austrian Empress, Maria Theresia, acquired the land in 1774 and planned to build a grand church. When she died in 1780, the money ran out and the chapel could not be furnished as richly as intended. It was 1841 before private donations and the Catholic Church provided the necessary funds for the interior to be completed.

MUSEUM OF DECORATIVE ARTS

A few metres east along Bredgade, you will see a typical Frederiksstaden rococo building (1754). Now home to the ★**Kunstindustrimuseet** ③③ (open Tues–Sun noon–4pm; Wed noon–6pm), it was a hospital until 1910 and in 1919 it became the Museum of Decorative and Applied Arts. The principal attractions here are the collection of *objets d'art*, some fine French rococo furniture, and various works by Danish designers. The library contains around 6,500 books and periodicals on art, costume and industrial design. Its pretty garden is an inviting place to stop for a rest.

TOWARDS NYBODER

Fredericiagade will take you away from Frederiksstaden. At 70 Store Kongensgade is Ida Davidsen, one of the best *frokost* restaurants in town *(see page 113)*.

The ★**Nyboder** district, with its humbler dwellings, forms quite a contrast to sophisticated Amalienborg. Nyboder was built in the 1730s

Star Attractions
● **Kunstindustrimuseet**
(Museum of Decorative
and Applied Arts)
● **Nyboder**

Medical Museum
For a fascinating glimpse of hospital life and medical treatment through the ages, the Medicinsk-Historisk Museum at 62 Bredgade, is housed in the old Surgical Academy founded in 1787 (guided tours only: Thur–Fri 11am and 1pm, Sun 1pm; in Danish).

Kunstindustrimuseet garden theatre

Map on page 44

Fogtdals Photocafé
Don't miss Fogtdals Photocafé, 22 Østergade, near Kongens Nytorv. Here, you can enjoy a coffee while looking at the latest photographic exhibition and watching the streetlife outside at the smart end of Strøget.

Below and bottom: aspects of Nyboder

for seafarers and their families, and some cottages in **Sankt Pauls Gade** (20–40) have retained their original design. They were built with one floor, but most of them have had extra floors added.

In Nyboder itself, the more recent buildings are finished in an ochre/yellow shade, while in Rævegade to the north, the dark grey brick facades reflect the prevailing fashions of the late 19th century.

The fascinating history of the Nyboder area is documented in the **Nyboder Mindestuer** ㉞ at Sankt Pauls Gade 20 (open Wed 11am–2pm, Sun 11am–4pm).

PEACEFUL ENCLAVE

Sankt Pauls Kirke (1877) near the museum is sometimes used as a venue for concerts. It is almost as if time has stood still on the church square. Rather reminiscent of Carlsberg's Humleby *(see page 31)*, there is a certain fragility about this quiet corner at the heart of a major European city. If you take a stroll around the area, you may come across Rosengade, one particularly idyllic retreat which certainly does justice to its 'green' name. During the next few years, it is intended that some of the street names be changed back to their original titles.

ISLAMIC ART AT DAVIDS SAMLING

Kronprinsessegade leads back to Rosenborg Have. If you pass the entrance to the park, you will spot a dark, rather severe-looking building, which will house a very special museum, **Davids Samling** ㉟ (closed for refurbishment until mid-2008). The museum was originally founded in 1945 to keep the art treasures that the lawyer, C.L. David, amassed.

As well as various European artworks and *objets d'art* from the 18th and 19th centuries, Scandinavia's finest collection of Islamic art will be displayed here, including glass and pottery, and book miniatures.

6: Along the West Bank

Nyhavn – Harbour promenade – Gefionspring-vand – Little Mermaid – Langeliniekaj – Fri-havnen – Kastellet – Frihedsmuseet

Map on page 44

Nowhere in Copenhagen has changed as much as the port area. The traditional industries, such as shipbuilding, commerce and maritime travel, have collapsed, and the B & W shipbuilding company, on the east side of the port, became insolvent in the 1990s, bringing to an end commercial activity in the city centre area. This tour shows what has become of the west side of the port. It follows the Langelinie coastal promenade – the old, defensive wall. While warehouses and quayside installations have had to make way for change, the Little Mermaid looks on contemplatively.

Below: anchor on the waterfront, in honour of sailors of World War II
Below: Nyhavn

Finish off the tour with a visit to the fascinating Freedom Museum, which documents the period of German occupation (1940–45). If you take a break in the pleasant quayside gardens, this will make a relaxing afternoon stroll – museum visits not included.

NYHAVN'S MARITIME PAST

Set out for Kongens Nytorv, accessible by bus no. 26 from City Hall Square. At the spot where a huge anchor honours Danish sailors killed in

Map on page 44

World War II, Kongens Nytorv joins the short ★★ **Nyhavn** harbour. The 'new' harbour was dug in 1671 to link Kongens Nytorv with the greater harbour. In those days, rows of tall houses lined both sides of the waterway, and in the warehouses and offices trade flourished. Sailors drank in the quayside taverns and, in its early days, Nyhavn was no place for respectable Copenhageners to take a quiet stroll.

The maritime atmosphere was appreciated by artists and writers. Celebrated former residents include composer Daniel F.R. Kuhlau who lived at No. 23, man of letters Georg Brandes at No. 18, and fairytale writer Hans Christian Andersen, who resided at No. 18, then No. 20 and, from 1848–67, at No. 67.

NYHAVN'S LIVELY NORTH BANK

Those tough times are now in the past, but the interest remains. Many of the facades on the sunny (northern) side of Nyhavn are painted in bright, friendly colours and, during the warmer months, the canal banks become a veritable hive of activity.

Nyhavn is host to a mixed range of restaurants. What attracts locals and tourists alike is the hustle and bustle against a background of proud sailing ships. On sunny days, crowds swarm along

Below: music on the canal
Bottom: seating at a premium

the northern bank and pour in and out of the bars. Small boats ply up and down the canal, which is a terminus for canalboat cruises, as well as a hydrofoil service to Sweden.

Star Attraction
● Nyhavn

VIEW FROM THE SOUTH BANK

Every visitor to Copenhagen will want to take home a snap of the bustling Nyhavn – and the best views are from the quieter south bank, where offices have largely replaced restaurants. Save the north side for an evening stroll, when it will probably be less frantic. You will pass in front of a side entrance to the baroque **Charlottenborg Slot**, since 1754 the home of the Royal Academy of Fine Arts (open daily 10am–5pm). The palace was built at the end of the 17th century, shortly after Kongens Nytorv.

> **Art at Charlottenborg**
> This former palace on Kongens Nytorv, now the Royal Academy of Fine Arts, is the venue for changing exhibitions of contemporary Danish and international art. Go through the front gate and into the back courtyard to find the exhibition area (open daily 10am–5pm).

EVERY BUILDING TELLS A STORY

The **Nyhavnsbro** will take you over to the north side of the canal. On the way through to the Øresund, it is worth stopping to look at the house entrances and facades. Plaques, statues and stucco adornments remind visitors of celebrated former inhabitants, including Hans Christian Andersen. Some diving equipment, a relic from the 'Svitzer' rescue company which used to be based here, adorns the house on the corner of **Kvæsthusgade**.

At the end of the canal, look out for **71 Nyhavn Hotel**, an impressive example of how an old warehouse (1805) can be preserved. Above the wide windows, formerly openings for goods, the beam for supporting the lifting tackle is still clearly visible.

Nyhavn north side at dusk

KVÆSTHUSBROEN FERRY DOCK

The last remnant of the Baltic shipping trade is the **Kvæsthusbroen** landing stage, the departure point for ferries to Bornholm. A new playhouse for the Royal Theatre will be erected on the site of the old ferry docks. It will lie almost opposite the new opera house. By the **Promenade** to the

Map
on page
44

north of Kvæsthusbroen peace returns. Many of the warehouses, some more than 200 years old, have been beautifully restored and have found new uses. The Copenhagen Admiral Hotel was once a grain store that itself developed out of two store-rooms in 1885.

THE WATERFRONT AT AMALIEHAVN

Occupying the adjoining space and enclosed in concrete and marble, **Amaliehavn** is a green space with a fountain (1983) that has never really been accepted by the local people. It is, however, a pleasant place to sit and watch the activity on the harbour and the new opera house. From here it is possible to view the Amalienborg Palace square to the west, and the unmistakable copper dome of the Marmorkirken *(see page 62)* beyond. Probably the best facility in this garden is the kiosk where walkers can buy an ice-cream, before continuing their stroll along the promenade.

Below: Amaliehavn
Bottom: Florentine-style warehouses

HOW SCULPTURES WERE CAST

The scene along this stretch would have been very different 200 hundred years ago, with sailing ships loading their cargo before setting off to Greenland or the Caribbean, and whalers returning from arduous trips on the North Sea. The three **Florentine-style warehouses** ❸ date from around that time. Two of them were converted into apartments in the 1970s. The ground floor of the third warehouse contains the Royal Casting Collection, **Den Kongelige Afstøbningssamling** (open Wed 2–8pm, Sun 2–5pm) with casts of sculptures from various eras. A replica of Michelangelo's *David* stands in front of the building.

THE GEFION FOUNTAIN

On the opposite side of the Sound lies the extensive **Holmen** district, which the army cleared in 1995 and is now undergoing major changes including the immense opera house donated to the city by Mærsk McKinney Møller, owner of

Mærsk. Pass the Customs House and carry on towards the terminal for the ferry to the Polish port of Swinoujscie. Behind a wrought-iron gate, some way inland, tourists often gather to admire Copenhagen's most spectacular fountain, the ★ **Gefionspringvand** ㊲.

The sculptor, Anders Bundgaard, took 11 years to complete this colossal masterpiece, which draws its inspiration from Nordic mythology. It symbolises the goddess, Gefion, who turned her four sons into bulls and attached them to a plough to drag the island of Sjælland away from the Swedish mainland.

Not far from the splashing waters of the fountain stands **St Alban's Church** in English-inspired Gothic. Built between 1885 and 1887, it served to strengthen the ties between the Danish and British royal families. In 1863 Alexandra, the oldest daughter of Denmark's Christian IX, married Edward, who later became King Edward VII of England. See the notice-board outside the church for opening times.

Below: the Gefion fountain
Bottom: a close-up view

THE LITTLE MERMAID

The Gefion Fountain marks the start of the Langelinie. Although this promenade is bordered by numerous sculptures, the prettiest, the most famous and now *the* symbol for Copenhagen is

Map
on page
44

Lille Havfrue, the ★★ **Little Mermaid** ㊳. Created by Edvard Eriksen and modelled on his wife, it depicts the tragic sea-maiden who exchanged her tail for legs in order to win the love of an earthly prince, as recounted in one of Hans Christian Andersen's fairytales.

Carl Jacobsen of Carlsberg Brewery fame commissioned the work and was responsible for specifying where it should be placed. It has graced the Langelinie since 1913. However, it is not the original accident-prone sculpture. At one time the head was sawn off, and later the arm, but fortunately the original moulds have been kept and replacements have been made.

In real life, the sculpture is significantly smaller than most photographs make it appear.

Below: the Little Mermaid
Bottom: skating along
the quay

LANGELINIEKAJ PROMONTORY

The 1-km (0.6-mile) long **Langeliniekaj** north of the yachting marina marks the end of the Langelinie. Built in 1894 at the same time as the neighbouring Frihavnen, it is the meeting point for modern cruise ships and antiquated freighters from all over the world.

For walkers, the best view of the comings and goings is from the raised, tree-lined promenade beside the asphalt track along the quay. This stretch of road is very popular with locals, who

on summer weekends drive their cars onto the promenade, look out over the Øresund and enjoy an ice-cream.

NEW LIFE FOR FRIHAVNEN

On the west side of the promenade lies the next destination. **Frihavnen** (Free Harbour) was completed in 1894. By the 1970s, the basin and facilities could no longer be used by modern freighters and container ships and so it was closed. Now it is a splendid example of how decaying industrial areas can be given a new lease of life.

Around the edge of the eastern harbour, a fine new office and residential area made from glass, concrete and brick has been completed and the area landscaped. One relic from the past remains: architect Dahlerup's ornate warehouse has been fully restored and now houses offices.

INLAND TO KASTELLET

Return to the city centre via the **Kastellet** or Citadel, a key element in the establishment of the Langelinie. This installation goes back to the middle of the 17th century when, after the loss of the southern Swedish provinces, the city boundaries had to be moved outside the gates as a defence against unwanted visitors *(see page 14)*.

Frederik III ordered the construction of the defensive wall and citadel to guard the harbour entrance. In 1664, the first soldiers took up their positions in the Frederikshavn citadel, which later became known simply as Kastellet. Ramparts and a moat surround the strictly symmetrical, star-shaped site.

POPULAR MARRIAGE VENUE

Leave the Frihavnen via the **Norgesport**. This grassy bank is now popular with mothers pushing pushchairs, dog-walkers and joggers, but the military is still there, too. Renovated at the end of the 1980s, the barracks are out of bounds for the general public. Nevertheless, the soldiers and the

Star Attraction
● **Little Mermaid**

> **Top designs**
> One of the most exciting aspects of the docklands rejuvenation is Paustian, a furniture store featuring the best in contemporary design from Denmark and abroad. It also houses a good restaurant. The architect of the waterfront building was Jørn Utzon, renowned for his Sydney Opera House design.

Keeping out the sun

Map on page 44

Map on page 44

Shopping in Østerbro
Small, speciality shops characterise the neighbourhood of Østerbro, just inland from Frihavnen. For organic foods visit Urtehuset on Østerbrogade and Den Økologiske Bager on Rosenvængets Allé. Pif Paf Puf on the corner of Vordingborggade and Strandboulevarden specialises in well-designed educational toys. Copenhagen's glass gallery, Galleri Grønlund, is at 6 Skt Jakobs Plads.

Statue of Frederik IX at the promenade along the waterfront

public live together in harmony. In fact, it is the citadel church (1705), of all places, that enjoys popularity with couples about to marry. Sometimes on a Saturday afternoon, traffic jams form as wedding guests arrive and depart.

Next to the church stands the detention centre (1725) where enemies of the state were held. Detainees have included traitors, disgraced dignitaries and, most recently, Werner Best, Hitler's commander in Denmark.

PREPARED FOR A SIEGE

On a section of the ramparts above the church stands the third version of the citadel's own windmill (1847).

This outpost was designed to be fully self-sufficient in the event of a siege, so the barracks did not just consist of accommodation and ammunition stores, but there were also tanks full of drinking water and even a bakery.

THE FREEDOM MUSEUM

A cobbled road links the Norgesport with the **Sjællandsport** in the south. On the other side of the moat, a memorial commemorates those Danes who died during the period of German occupation (1940–45). It also marks the point where you can cross to Churchillparken, the location for the ★★**Frihedsmuseet** ㊳ (open May–Sept: Tues–Sat 10am–4pm, Sun 10am–5pm; Oct–Apr: Tues–Sat 10am–3pm, Sun 10am–4pm).

This museum documents the activities of the Danish Resistance Movement during the German occupation, 1940–45 *(see page 15)*. Displays illustrate the daring exploits of the Danish activists, who spirited Jews across the border to Sweden, manned radio stations and operated printing presses.

Others made weapons, committed acts of sabotage or fought alongside the Allied Forces. Period documents and newspaper cuttings show how the occupying forces reacted to the resistance movement.

7: A Break from the City

Gammel Dok – Christianshavn Kanal – Vor Frelsers Kirke – Free State of Christiania – Christians Kirke

The bridge by the old Stock Exchange on Slotsholmen leads across the Inderhavn into the Christianshavn district, where the pace of life visibly slows. But you will soon see that modern building styles have spread across the water, a fact demonstrated by the singularly unattractive Foreign Ministry. To the southwest a whole new quarter has been built on the premises of the former shipyard Burmeister and Wain.

A FREE STATE IN THE CITY

Around the quiet Christianshavn Kanal, the landscape remains unchanged, although a whiff of decay pervades the air in some places. This area is home to many ordinary as well as some extraordinary folk.

In the Free State of Christiania, the 2001 30th anniversary celebrations highlighted the sometimes troubled, yet mainly successful, life of the area that started in the 1970s as a social experiment on the site of an abandoned 19th-century barracks. Despite hostility from the city authorities and prophecies of doom, the majority of

Map on page 74

Star Attraction
● Frihedsmuseet

Below: waterfront lunch
Bottom: cruising the canal

Map below

Danes have voted to retain Christiania's independence. This tour lasts around three hours.

Across to Christianshavn

Christianshavn Canal

Take bus no. 2A from the city centre. The **Knippelsbro** bridges the Inderhavnen, the channel between the city centre and Christianshavn. Just to the left stand the bleak, grey offices of the Danish Foreign Ministry (1980) – this huge complex by Asiatisk Plads has little in common with the rest of Christianshavn. The adjoining **Strandgade** provides clear evidence of how this quarter looked in its earlier days.

Harbour Project

Four hundred years ago, this area was nothing but marshland with a few small islands. In order to create a harbour, between 1617 and 1622 thousands of tree trunks were driven into the soil, much earth was shifted, and a rectangular settlement created and named Christianshavn after the then king, Christian IV. A canal was dug in

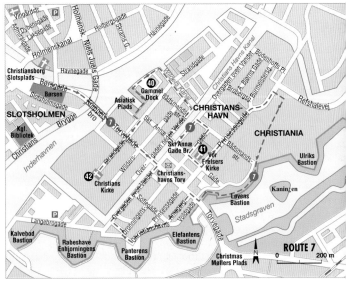

the Dutch style to divide the area into an upper and a lower town. Initially, Christianshavn was an independent municipality, but in 1682 it was annexed to Copenhagen, whereupon the settlement was extended and the unprotected east side was enclosed by a semi-circular wall.

EVIDENCE OF PROSPERITY

As the city's trading links developed at the beginning of the 18th century, new warehouses, offices, docks and workshops were built at the water's edge. **Asiatisk Plads** owes its name to the 'Asiatisk Kompagni', whose premises were grouped around a small harbour basin.

On the north side of the square, the marble facade of the elongated rococo warehouse (designed by Nicolai Eigtved in 1750) dates from Christianshavn's heyday. Now fashionably restored, it is used as a conference centre.

Until 1918, a harbour lay on the other long side of the warehouse, but this was filled in. Today a car park occupies the site of Copenhagen's first dry dock (1739) for the repair and maintenance of sailing ships.

GAMMEL DOK

Little remains of the ★ **Gammel Dok** , the Old Dock, apart from its name. Sadly, despite all the restored warehouses, the quayside is unable to recreate the old maritime atmosphere. No wooden sailing boats are moored alongside and no old sea-dogs sit by the water's edge with pipe in mouth.

Only the excellent cafeteria in the Gammel Dok can offer any sustenance, and that will be from a salad counter rather than a smoky old sailors' bar.

In the mid-1980s, the neighbouring warehouse (1882) was impressively restored. Unlike many similar projects, the public have access to the interior, as it belongs to the **Dansk Arkitektur Center** and is used as a venue for exhibitions (Danish Centre for Architecture, open daily 10am–5pm). With its bright rooms, exposed beams and newly laid wooden floors, there could

Star Attraction
● Gammel Dok

Early terraces
Although this quarter is considerably younger than the centre of Copenhagen, it contains some of the city's oldest terraced houses. A good example of these early buildings are Nos. 26–36 Strandgade, although admittedly new floors have been added and the frontages altered.

Old ships, modern developments

Below and bottom: the Danish Centre for Architecture, and detail

Map on page 74

be no better example of how to renovate an old building. From the quayside, the view encompasses Slotsholmen, with the old Stock Exchange in the foreground. The 60-year-old Knippelsbro occupies the same site as all the other bridges that have linked the old town and Christianshavn.

CHRISTIANSHAVN KANAL

Much more of a waterside feel surrounds the ★ **Christianshavn Kanal**, where rows of pleasure boats bob up and down. The closer you get to the **Wildersbro** bridge on the east side of Gammel Dok, the more evidence there is of better bygone days.

On the right-hand side stands the orange-yellow **Pakhus 4**, another example of a successful conversion from warehouse to office block. Many of the facades in this quarter exhibit the same gaudy colour scheme. In the early 18th century, the opposite side of the canal was occupied by the premises of ship owner and timber-merchant Andreas Bjørn.

The brick building in red and yellow housed the offices, the half-timbered structure next door was the sail-making workshop, while the company's own wharf suffered the same fate as the Gammel Dok and was filled in.

THE UPPER AND LOWER TOWNS

Take a right turn and follow the main canal which splits Christianshavn in half. The two narrow lanes on either side of the water, **Overgaden neden Vandet** (Lower Town) and **Overgaden oven Vandet** (Upper Town) are lined with more old warehouses, town houses and company headquarters. Rather than examining the various facades, it is perhaps more interesting to view the canal from the Skt Annæ Gade bridge.

The boats tied up against the tree-lined banks make a picturesque sight, probably one of the most photogenic in Copenhagen. It is a relaxing spot where you could easily forget about the pulsating capital city only a few hundred metres

Opera House

The Copenhagen Opera House, Operaen, is situated on the harbour front at Holmen. Designed by Danish architect Henning Larsen and opened in 2005, it is topped by a spectacular 'floating' roof. Opera, ballet and classical music performances are staged here and guided tours are also available (Mon–Wed 10am–4pm; tel 33 69 69 69; www.operahus.dk).

away, were it not for the multi-lingual commentaries emanating from the tourist boats which pass underneath the bridge.

LOCAL BENEFACTOR

From the bridge, turn left into Overgaden oven Vandet and look out for No. 48. Peter Norden Sølling's portrait on the frontage was the work of Thorvald Bindebøll, son of the Slotsholmen architect, M.G. Bindebøll. The effects of the British bombardment *(see page 15)* disturbed Sølling, a generous man, and in 1819 he set up a fund to support the widows and families of seamen. He collected the money in the cylinder of a bomb which the British had fired, and this explains why the foundation went under the name of *Bombebøssen* ('bomb tin').

In 1891 No. 48 Overgaden oven Vandet became the new home of the foundation, and the building has remained unaltered ever since, although the foundation is now based in the parallel Dronningensgade.

The elongated rococo building at Overgaden 58–64 has undergone many changes and has been put to numerous uses since it was built in 1754. After starting out as a school, it then served as a prison, a hospital and a rehabilitation centre for wounded naval personnel. It is now

Star Attraction
● Christianshavn Kanal

> **Coffee break**
> If you feel a few pangs of hunger and decide that you want more than just a quiet contemplative moment, take a few steps along Skt Annæ Gade, as far as the corner of Wildersgade, and call in for a mid-morning snack at the 'Café Wilder' *(see page 113)*, a popular haunt of the younger crowd.

Relaxing by the canal

Map on page 74

the **Orlogsmuseet** (Royal Danish Naval Museum, open Tues–Sun noon–4pm; free admission on Wed), where models of ships from the 17th century, uniforms, nautical instruments and weapons are housed. Probably the museum's most prized exhibit is the tiny submarine, which visitors can enter.

Below: Orlogsmuseet facade
Bottom: view from the spire of Vor Frelsers Kirke

VOR FRELSERS KIRKE

Return to Skt Annæ Gade and on the left stands the imposing ★★ **Vor Frelsers Kirke** ④ (Our Saviour's Church, open Apr–Aug: Mon–Sat 11am–4.30pm, Sun noon–4.30pm; Sept–Mar: Mon–Sat 11am–3.30pm, Sun noon–3.30pm; tower closed Nov–Mar).

Situated in this modest quarter, Vor Frelsers Kirke's opulent interior comes as something of a surprise. The church was built between 1682 and 1696 in baroque style.

Among the most striking features are the monumental church organ, supported by two large stucco elephants (1698) and the altar with its marble plinth (1732).

The spire (1752), with its external staircase, is a striking landmark and, if time permits, the climb to the top is well worth the effort, providing one of the finest views over Copenhagen. To make the ascent requires an exciting expedition through intricate roof timbers.

FREE STATE OF CHRISTIANIA

The unusual freedom statue on the corner of Prinsessegade and Bådsmandsstræde hints at a change of atmosphere in this city quarter. Just 100 metres (110 yds) northeast along Prinsessegade appears the entrance to the **★★ Free State of Christiania**.

When in 1971 the Danish military abandoned the barracks on Bådsmandsstræde, property speculators started to rub their hands in anticipation, but their hopes of a quick profit were dashed when a group of alternative types, drop-outs and hippies moved in and sought to realise their idealistic notion of communal living.

For 16 years, the properties were threatened with demolition, but in 1987 the Danish Parliament gave its approval to the self-appointed Free State, subject to the signing of an agreement about how the land could be used, as it still belongs to the Defence Ministry.

DANES GIVE THEIR SUPPORT

The agreements have been signed, but conservative circles continue to display hostility to the residents of Christiania, though in the late 1990s, more than 60 percent of Danes voted to preserve the free town. Critics complain primarily about the much reduced sale and use of marijuana and argue that the inhabitants represent a permanent threat to law and order.

Despite this, Christiania now seems more secure than ever. This traffic-free area, with its generous provision of nurseries and playgrounds, is certainly ideal for children, who make up a large percentage of the inhabitants.

Bicycles and restored ovens are exported to many parts of Europe, and the 'Grønne Hal' market recycles building materials. The Loppen concert hall is a lively cultural centre, and the Spiseloppen (The Eating Flea) restaurant is among the best in the city.

The democratically-elected assembly has made some difficult decisions: to counter the drug-pushers, the Christianiers have banned the sale and

Star Attractions
● **Vor Frelsers Kirke**
● **Free State of Christiania**

Art in the Free State
Christiania's brightly painted buildings and eclectic designs are a joyful sight after the more sedate architecture of the city. Murals, rainbows and spiritual figures decorate houses, restaurants and converted barrack blocks.

Below: the Free State of Christiania
Bottom: Christiania buskers

Top: no drugs

Below: Christianshavns Voldgade
Bottom: mural in Christiana

consumption of hard drugs and have evicted a gang of rockers who sought to gain control of the area.

CHRISTIANIA WALKING TOUR

Visitors are invited to come and share a vegetarian meal, to take part in the community's cultural life or to stroll along the Stadsgraven moat. Cameras aren't particularly welcome. The best way to explore the Free State of Christiania is by joining an organised walking tour (Sat and Sun at 3pm). There is an informative tourist guide, *Nitten*, with text in English.

You can continue along the ramparts straight from Christiania. **Christianshavns Vold** runs between Stadsgraven and **Christianshavns Voldgade** and provides a good overall view of the site. Only the Torvegade over to Amager interrupts the zigzag line of the ramparts, with its five-cornered bastions, where the soldiers once stood guard.

AROUND TORVEGADE

The 100-metre (110-yd) **Amagergade**, a turning off Torvegade which runs parallel to Voldgade, used to be the poorest street in the quarter. In the mid-19th century, almost 1,000 people were crammed into

the insanitary dwellings, and tuberculosis and other diseases were rife. Standing in front of these neat half-timbered houses today, it is hard to imagine the misery that the people had to endure.

Heading west from Amagergade, the ramparts, canal and Overgaden oven Vandet converge. On the corner of Sofiegade is Sofies Kælder, an underground bar from which cheery mainstream jazz echoes every Sunday.

CHRISTIANS KIRKE

At the westernmost end of Strandgade sits the ★ **Christians Kirke 42** (open Mar–Oct: daily 8am–6pm; otherwise 8am–5pm). It was built between 1755 and 1759 at the same time as the grand buildings in Frederiksstaden, hence the familiar rococo style.

Rather like a theatre, it has three galleries with boxes, which were set aside for the district's wealthy families.

OLD DOCKYARDS

Next to the church, where a new office block now occupies the best waterside location, were the dockyards of **Burmeister & Wain**, or B & W as the company was known.

In 1996, precisely 150 years after it was established, B & W went into liquidation. Paddle steamers, ferries, luxury yachts, cruise liners, warships, container vessels and supertankers all slid off the slipway here.

Despite a reputation for quality, the Danes could not compete against the low-wage economies of the Far East. B & W's vast yards on the island of Refshaleøen, north of Christianshavn, are now quiet.

The history of B & W can be followed at the Diesel House (Elvaerksvej 50; open Mon–Fri and 1st Sun of month 10am–4pm; tel: 32 54 02 27) situated south of the city at Vasbygade. The museum is built around a B&W diesel engine from 1932, which was once the largest diesel engine in the world.

Star Attraction
● Christians Kirke

Where to shop
Torv and Torvegade are the main shopping streets of Christianshavn, with the Christianshavn Torv marketplace on Torvegade (look out for the ancient, unused telephone kiosk).

Below and bottom: Christians Kirke detail and interior

Map on page 83

8: Frederiksberg

Københavns Bymuseum – Det Kongelige Danske Haveselskabs Have – Frederiksberg Have – Zoologisk Have – Royal Copenhagen Porcelain Factory Shop

Close to the City Museum runs the border between Copenhagen and Frederiksberg, a town within a town with a population of about 90,000. Unlike nearby Vesterbro, this area used to be favoured by the middle and upper classes, but it is now hard to tell the difference between Frederiksberg and Copenhagen. Visitors are particularly attracted to its extensive parks which surround the now fully restored Frederiksberg Palace. This is where Copenhagen Zoo is situated. Set aside a good half-day for this tour, longer if you intend to visit the zoo.

Monument to reform
As you set off for Frederiksberg, behind Tivoli Gardens and in front of the Central Station, you will pass by the 15-metre (50-ft) high sandstone Frihedsstøtten (1792–97), a column recalling the agricultural reforms of the 18th century which ended serfdom.

EN ROUTE TO FREDERIKSBERG

Take bus no. 26 from City Hall Square or Tivoli Gardens and alight near the City Museum at 59 Vesterbrogade. The more energetic may prefer to get around by bike.

Kobenhavns Bymuseum: old posters

THE CITY MUSEUM

★ **Københavns Bymuseum 44** (open Mon–Thurs 10am–4pm, Wed–10am–9pm) occupies the former premises of the Royal Shooting Club (1786) on Vesterbrogade in the north of Vesterbro.

The City Museum's exhibits are particularly impressive for their originality and credibility as, unusually for a town museum, they focus not only on the glory days of the city's past, but also on the difficult periods in its development. It looks closely, for example, at Copenhagen around the middle of the 18th century, when, within the space of only a few decades, the population doubled. A smaller department is devoted to Søren Kierkegaard, the father of existentialism.

A clay model outside the museum shows what the city would have looked like around 1530, and the nearby cobbled **Absalonsgade** has been turned into a museum street, where lanterns, fire hydrants and an art nouveau telephone kiosk covered with original advertising posters revive the atmosphere of the early 20th century.

SØREN KIERKEGAARD EXHIBITION

A small exhibition in Københavns Bymuseum celebrates the intellectual contributions of the philosopher Søren Kierkegaard, one of the city's most famous sons.

Model of the city around 1530, outside Københavns Bymuseum

BLOOMS IN A ROYAL GARDEN

You will cross the boundary between Copenhagen and Frederiksberg just after the bus turns into **Frederiksberg Allé**, formerly Frederik IV's private road to his palace in Frederiksberg. It was 1862 before ordinary citizens were allowed to use this boulevard, which is lined by some fine patrician houses. Leave the bus before it has turned the corner, and in front of you stands the gateway into **Frederiksberg Have**, a green lung in the heart of the city.

Before passing through the iron gates between the two lodges, it is worth making a short detour to the left. This small park, ★ **Det Kongelige Danske Haveselskabs Have ㊺** (the Garden of the Royal Danish Garden Society) is divided into several sections, representing different types of landscaped gardens. It is a colourful, fastidiously

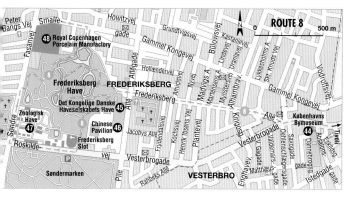

Map
on page
83

tended, delightfully scented jewel, where many delights await the visitor.

FREDERIKSBERG HAVE

After the centrally located Kongens Have (King's Garden) next to Rosenborg Slot *(see page 55)*, the Copenhageners' favourite park is the spacious **★★Frederiksberg Have** (open daily from 6am until sunset. Chinese pavilion: May–Sept: Sun 2–4pm).

Inspired by many journeys to France and Italy, Frederik IV had the gardens laid out symmetrically in baroque style. **Frederiksberg Palace**, built in 1703, overlooks the park from a hill in the south of the grounds. The palace has undergone several facelifts since it was built and is now the home of the Danish army's Officers' Training School. It is open to visitors for guided tours the last Sat of each month (excluding July and Dec) at 11am and 1pm.

Below: lazy days in Frederiksberg Have
Bottom: Frederiksberg Palace

EXPLORING THE PARK

The gardens were redesigned in an English style at the end of the 18th century, and Frederik's moats were dug out later and linked together to form a system of canals, so that in the summer visitors can enjoy a relaxing boat trip through the park.

Crocuses, lilies, rhododendron, roses and lavender keep Frederiksberg Have in colour throughout the summer months, but more flowerbeds, huge trees, a fountain, artificial caves and little waterfalls add to its appeal. Families picnic and groups of children play on the grass, while sun-worshippers bask on regardless of all the chatter and laughter.

On an island in the lake stands a pretty **Chinese pavilion** ㊻, where in the 19th century Frederik VI brought his family together to take afternoon tea with him.

Skating is proving a popular winter pastime among Copenhageners and, along with Tivoli Gardens, a rink is set up annually at the main entrance to Frederiksberg Have. Skates can be hired by the hour.

ACROSS TO SØNDERMARKEN

Opposite the entrance to the palace lies **Søndermarken,** a continuation of the Frederiksberg green belt. Between 1856 and 1859, what is now level grass was turned into several ponds, because the city was growing rapidly and the population faced serious water shortages. Here you can visit **Cisternerne**, the Museum of Modern Glass Art, located in underground water reservoirs dating back to 1850 (open Thur–Fri 2–6pm, Sat–Sun 11am–5pm).

POLAR BEARS AT THE ZOO

Copenhagen Zoo, the ★ **Zoologisk Have** ⓗ (open daily 9am–5pm) is located in the southwest corner of Frederiksberg Have. At the entrance stands a mini-version of the Eiffel Tower which can be climbed for a few *kroner*. Inside the zoo, the polar bears steal the show. The seal and penguin enclosures are also extremely popular at feeding time, and there is a corner where young children can stroke the animals. Exhibitions, models and dioramas complete the show.

FLORA AND FAUNA IN THE PARK

You can explore yet more of Frederiksberg Have while en route north towards the next destina-

Star Attraction
● Zoo

Danish fare
In the eastern section of Frederiksberg Have are three Familiehaver (family gardens), accessible only from Pile Allé, where you can enjoy typical Danish cuisine in the open air between mid-May and mid-September.

Attention-seeking toucan

Map
on page
83

Not just china
As well as china, the shop at the Royal Copenhagen Porcelain Factory also sells crystal glass in modern designs produced by another member of the Royal Copenhagen group, Holmegaard. The glassworks, founded in 1825, are at Fensmark in southern Sjaelland.

tion. There are some fine linden trees on the **Mathildehøj** and a colony of herons on **Andebakkeøen Island**.

ROYAL COPENHAGEN PORCELAIN

When you reach Smallegade, turn left at the crossing for the entrance to the ★ **Royal Copenhagen Porcelain Factory Shop** ⓭ (in Søndre Fasanvej 9; open Mon–Fri 10am–5.30pm, Sat 10am–2pm, *see also page 45*).

THE PORCELAIN WORKS

The Porcelain Works used to be here but is now outside the city. The products are very intricate and almost a third of the employees are artists. To be able to paint one of the costlier items, the craftsmen must undergo a full seven years of training. Some pieces require more than 1,000 brushstrokes.

Royal Copenhagen Porcelain

ROYAL DESIGNS

Royal Copenhagen 'Blue Fluted' dinner services have been in production virtually unchanged since 1775. The painting method is the same as that used on Meissen pottery, and that in turn originated in China. Experience proved that cobalt blue retained its colour well during the firing process. 'Flora Danica' (1789) is another well-known pattern. This new design was ordered by King Christian VII as a present for the Russian tsarina, Katharina II, but she died before the 1,800-piece set was finished. The motifs of the natural world were taken from *Flora Danica*, the Danish botanical encyclopaedia.

FACTORY SHOP BARGAINS

Although the products are mainly china for everyday use, due to the very high quality prices are expensive, but you do have the opportunity to visit the factory shop, which sells seconds discounted at between 30 and 40 percent.

9. The Island of Amager

Amager – the city's offshore island
Kalvebod Fælled – Kongelunden – Søvang –
Dragør – Store Magleby – Amager Beach

For centuries, the 65-sq km (25-sq mile) island of Amager has supplied farm produce to the Danish capital. Paradoxically, Copenhagen has said thank you by creating a series of environmental problems on what was formerly a quiet retreat for its inhabitants. First of all, there is Kastrup airport with its noisy aeroplanes landing and taking off, then there is the high volume of both airport traffic and vehicles using the new Øresund bridge to

Map
below

Star Attraction
● **Porcelain Factory**

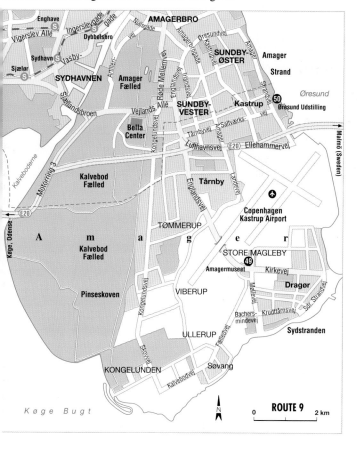

ROUTE 9

Map on page 87

Below: taking it easy
Bottom: Amager Fælled
Nature Reserve

Sweden. Nevertheless, the southern part of the island is blessed with fascinating nature reserves and also many pretty villages. To make the most of this tour, take a car or a bike. The new Ørestad and the metro has drastically changed the island and you will see new buildings being erected everywhere.

Amager is one of the up-and-coming parts of Copenhagen. To the east the beach is being developed and new housing is appearing everywhere. Close to the city centre the quarter called Islands Brugge has changed from a dull working class area to a hip and vivid place with a bustling waterfront and lots of cafés and bars. Not to mention the many modern art galleries like Nicolai Wallner. You get there by crossing Langebro close to City Hall Square.

Bus no. 33 also covers most of the route. If you like exploring, then allow a full day. Set out from the Bella Center in the heart of the new Ørestad, you can go there by metro.

KALVEBOD FÆLLED RESERVE

One kilometre (about ½ mile) beyond the Bella Center, the Kongelundsvej branches off the main road and crosses the motorway. This new route cuts across the flat and uncultivated **Kalvebod Fælled** in the west of the island.

For a period after World War II, Kalvebod Fælled, largely marshland drained by ditches, was used throughout the year as a training ground for Danish troops. It then became a bird and nature reserve, and its network of paths is ideal for cyclists and energetic walkers, but take a good map as it is inadequately signposted. In addition, parts of the reserve are out of bounds as the army left behind countless unexploded shells.

The new motorway has reduced the area of this unspoilt reserve quite considerably, but environmentalists hope that the bird-life will not be affected. Kestrels, buzzards, short-eared owls, hen-harriers and many other bird species either overwinter here or stay for the whole year. The car park by Frieslandsvej is a good starting place from which to explore the region. Alternatively, you can combine a tour of the Kalvebod Fælled with the neighbouring Kongelunden woodlands.

THE KING'S FOREST

Until about 200 years ago, Amager had few trees, so firewood and timber for construction work were always in short supply. Then several areas near **Kongelunden** were turned into forest. The land passed to the king in 1836, and he set up wild pheasant farms so that wealthy Copenhageners could enjoy a day's shooting. In 1920, the King's Forest was opened to the public, and walkers are still likely to encounter pheasants scratching around in the undergrowth.

The memorial near the car park and bus stop remembers one of the royal hunters. Straight forest tracks run westward towards the Amager coastline and the treeless coastal strips, where in autumn birds gather before heading south. It is possible to gain access to the larger Kalvebod Fælled reserve via an embankment to the north-west of the woodland.

COASTAL PATH

Cyclists can take the coastal path from **Søvang** to Dragør and enjoy the splendid views. In

Star Attraction
● Dragør

Shrovetide celebrations
Sixteenth-century Dutch farmers who settled around Dragør brought with them a lively Shrovetide custom that can still be seen today: men in fancy dress costumes ride horses at full speed, lances outstretched, to spear a barrel which is suspended over the course and split it in half.

Dragør: a day at the beach

Map on page 87

Søvang, smart, highly desirable seaside cottages with neat gardens overlook the Øresund, and in the summer the beach here is very popular with bathers.

> ### A day out in Sweden
> Ferries still ply their way across the Øresund, but with the opening of the new bridge, Malmö, Sweden's third city, is now a mere 35-minute train ride from Copenhagen Central Station. The free events magazine *Copenhagen This Week* has a section devoted to what's on across the water, and the Tourist Information Office at Malmö station can supply maps, brochures and advise on tours (tel: 040 34 12 00).

DRAGØR

The picturesque town of ★★ **Dragør** is the main attraction on Amager. Once a busy fishing and commercial port, it is now almost a living museum.

Diagonally opposite stands the oldest house in the town (1682), which is now the **Dragør Museum** of local history (open May–Sept: Tues–Sun noon–4pm).

On more than one occasion, fires have badly damaged the Old Town – the last was in 1988 – but every time the architects and builders manage to bring it back to life, ensuring that the reconstruction merges with the pretty, yellow-painted cottages.

DUTCH FARMS ON AMAGER

The **Amagermuseet ㊾** in **Store Magleby** in Hovedgaden (open May–Sept: Tues–Sun noon–4pm; Oct–Apr: Wed–Sun noon–4pm) reflects the Dutch influence on the island.

Amagermuseet, traditional costume display

In the 1520s Christian II brought Dutch farmers – noted for their farming expertise – to Amager to ensure that Copenhagen was always well supplied with farm produce. The two thatched farmsteads provide an appropriate setting for the agricultural collection.

ØRESUND BRIDGE

The impressive 16-km (10-mile) long road and rail bridge that links Copenhagen with Malmö in Sweden, providing a speedy route between the European mainland and Scandinavia, opened in 2000. It is the world's longest cable-stayed bridge of its kind, and is at the heart of a new development region which spans both sides of the water.

Excursion 1: The North

Experimentarium – Danmarks Akvarium – Charlottenlund Slotspark – Charlottenlund Strandpark – Bakken – Jægersborg Dyrehave

Map below

The northern districts of Gentofte, Charlottenlund and Klampenborg are where most wealthy Copenhageners live. Strandvejen, the coast road that runs beside the Øresund as far as Helsingør, is lined with grand villas, usually set back behind a wide green strip.

This area is by no means an exclusive enclave for the better-off. As well as an attractive golf

Map on page 91

course, yachting marinas and a racetrack, numerous other places offer rest and recreation to everyone, whatever the size of their pocket.

EXPERIMENTARIUM

Below: the Experimentarium
Bottom: aural exhibit

The ★**Experimentarium** (open Mon, Wed–Fri 9.30am–5pm, Tues 9.30am–9pm, Sat and Sun 11am–5pm; bus no. 1A from Central Station) is situated in the northern district of Hellerup in a wing of Copenhagen's last Tuborg brewery. It sets out to explain a variety of scientific principles, frequently using hands-on techniques.

The enormous 4,000sq metre (43,000sq ft) hall contains some 300 working exhibits sponsored by the private sector.

SCIENCE AT YOUR FINGERTIPS

'Learn by doing' is the message for everyone; you can test the capacity of your lungs, devise a calorie plan to suit your own body, carry out a drinking-water test, establish the radioactivity of naturally-occurring substances, or look at various ways of saving energy. Cell research, communication and data transfer, air and water, energy and environmental protection, nutrition and the workings of various human organs are just some of the topics which the inquisitive visitor can

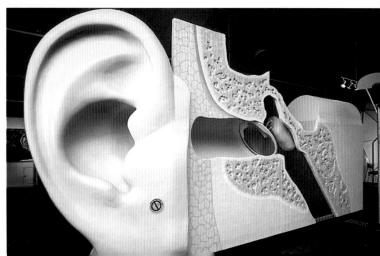

explore. Special educational programmes have been devised and so school parties make up most of the visitors on weekdays. Temporary exhibitions – with experimentation as the main theme – are also held during the year.

Star Attractions
- ● **Experimentarium**
- ● **Danmarks Akvarium**

SEALIFE AT DENMARK'S AQUARIUM

In a country like Denmark, which is surrounded by the sea, aquaria are quite common, but the ★ **Danmarks Akvarium** (open May–Aug: 10am–6pm; Sept–Oct and Feb–Apr: 10am–5pm; Nov–Jan 10am–4pm; S-train to Charlottenlund station, then an 800-metre (875-yd) walk via Jægersborg Allé or bus no. 14 from Rådhuspladsen) remains unique.

Beautifully designed pools contain marine fauna from all over the world. Large landscaped tanks, which require the filtration of 300,000 litres (66,000 gallons) of water, recreate those distant continents, where piranha fish bare their frightening teeth or motionless crocodiles await the arrival of their next meal.

As well as attempting to provide the fish and reptiles with their natural habitat, the aquarium also seeks to enlighten visitors by explaining some of the residents' little quirks. What, for example, are the secrets of the snapping turtle, why and how does the electric eel transmit electric impulses, or why does the huge sea bass seem so unperturbed by the narrow confines of its tank?

CHARLOTTENLUND CASTLE

Denmark's aquarium is situated in **Charlottenlund Slotspark**, by Strandvejen. The baroque castle was commissioned by Frederik IV for his daughter Charlotte Amalie in 1730, but the striking dome was not added until 1881.

Charlottenlund Fort, on the other side of Strandvejen, was built between 1886 and 1888 as part of a fortification system to protect the entrance to Copenhagen's harbour. Abandoned in 1932, the site was integrated into the new **Charlottenlund Strandpark**, now one of the

> **Ordrupgaard Gallery**
> While in Charlottenlund, don't miss the charming ★★ **Ordrupgaard Art Gallery** (110 Vilvordevej; open Tues–Sun noon–4pm). This noted collection of 19th and 20th-century French paintings by the likes of Degas, Renoir and Monet, and Danish work by artists such as Lyndbye and Hammershøi, was amassed by a businessman, Wilhelm Hansen, and bequeathed to the state in 1951.

Danmarks Akvarium

Map on page 91

All the fun of the fair
Few tourists find their way to Bakken, but as a straightforward funfair, it draws Copenhageners from all walks of life. Unlike many such fairs, the food on offer at Bakken is generally well regarded. Admission is free and the average cost of rides and food is well below that at Tivoli in the city centre.

Below: Charlottenlund Strandpark
Bottom: souvenir hats, Bakken

most popular beaches on Sjælland. Part of it also serves as a campsite in the summer.

BAKKEN FUNFAIR

The elegant suburb of Klampenborg is bordered to the north by a large, wooded area and the ★ **Bakken** pleasure park (open end-Mar–Aug: daily 2pm–midnight; July noon–midnight; S-train to Klampenborg station and then 800 metres (875 yds) on foot via the Dyrehavsvej or bus no. 14 from Rådhuspladsen). This site, with its proud, 400-year-old tradition, lies close to **Kirsten Pils Kilde**, a spring whose water was said to have contained medicinal powers. A market offering food, drink and entertainment was established near the spring. It later moved to a hill that gave its name to the fair.

Bakken is perhaps more of a genuine funfair than Tivoli; it is certainly less sophisticated. Pierrot, the clown, awaits the children in his little cabin, and performers and musicians play on the open-air stage. The other 100 or so attractions include a roller-coaster, dodgems, swing-boats, white-water rides, shooting-ranges, modern rides and amusement arcades.

ROYAL DEER PARK

Bakken Hill forms the southern edge of what used to be the royal hunting grounds, ★ **Jægersborg Dyrehave**. Frederik III was happy with a small reserve, but his son, Christian V, was a keen hunter, and after his coronation in 1670, he enlarged the grounds so that prey could be rounded up and driven towards the hunters. Forestry workers and hunters throughout Denmark were obliged to catch red deer and bring them to Jægersborg Dyrehave. The monarch's passion for hunting was to be his downfall – he died in a hunting accident in 1699.

In 1756 Frederik V opened up the spacious woodland to the public. Many of the trees, mainly beeches, oaks and other deciduous species, are more than 200 years old and stand a good 50 metres (165ft) high. Dyrehave, now the biggest recreational area within greater Copenhagen, is criss-crossed by a network of footpaths, bridle paths and wide tracks. During the summer you can take a ride through the forest in a horse-drawn carriage. Starting out from Bakken funfair, the fare is very reasonable.

OPEN-AIR THEATRE

If you feel like exploring the area on foot, keep left at the horse-drawn carriages, carry on for a few metres and you will pass the Kirsten Pils Kilde spring. At the second junction, turn right. A little further on, the **Ulvedalene** valley opens out on the left. This area was used as an open-air theatre from 1910 to 1949. In 1996, the tradition was revived for the Cultural Capital of Europe festivities, and the national drama *Elverhøj (see page 107)* was performed here, it has since continued.

VIEW FROM THE HUNTING LODGE

Turn right, left and right again at the subsequent cross-roads, and follow a wide track as far as the **Eremitagen** hunting lodge (1736). The splendid view from this hilltop extends over the Øresund and there is also a chance that you will see red deer grazing. Two paths downhill, parallel to the track, will bring you back to Bakken.

Star Attractions
● **Bakken funfair**
● **Jægersborg Dyrehave**

Below: Eremitagen
Bottom: Jaegeraborg Dyrehave

Map on page 91

Excursion 2: North Sjælland

Karen Blixen Museet – Louisiana Museum for Moderne Kunst – Frederiksborg Slot – Roskilde Domkirke – Vikingeskibsmuseet – Arken Museet for Moderne Kunst

If you have only a week to spend in Copenhagen, then you will have to be selective. But if you're in the city for two weeks, then you'll certainly have time for one or two day trips out into the Sjælland hinterland.

Below: Karen Blixen on safari in Africa
Bottom: Louisiana sculptures

KAREN BLIXEN AT RUNGSTEDLUND

The author, Karen Blixen (1885–1962), was the sort of person who courted controversy. In her work she was not concerned with social or psychological realism. For her, the questions that mattered were, 'Why is man on earth?' or 'What does God want from man?' Although Blixen's stylised language is not easy to penetrate, the success of her books demonstrates that she struck a chord with her readers. But many Danes disdained the baroness's superior attitude. Blixen insisted on being addressed by her title, she always dressed elegantly and spoke in a strictly correct, rather old-fashioned style. It is often forgotten, however, that she was one of the first Danes to take issue on women's rights.

From 1914 to 1931 Blixen lived as a coffee grower in East Africa, where she wrote her most successful novels. When she returned to Denmark, she settled at her parents' home in **Rungstedlund**, north of Copenhagen. In 1991 the house was converted into the **★ Karen Blixen Museet** (open May–Sept: Tues–Sun 10am–5pm; Oct–Apr: Wed–Fri 1–4pm, Sat and Sun 11am–4pm; S-train to Lyngby, then bus no. 388), which sheds light on the intriguing personality of Denmark's most celebrated female literary figure.

LOUISIANA MUSEUM OF MODERN ART

In the mid-1950s, the cheesemaker Knud W. Jensen walked the length of the Øresund coast in search of a suitable spot to realise his life-long dream. By his mid-40s, after successfully running a cheese factory, he was looking towards the art world for a new career. He bought a summer villa and parkland near Humlebæk, 40km (25 miles) north of Copenhagen, and began work on his project. Since 1958, **★★★ Louisiana Museum for Moderne Kunst** (open daily 10am–5pm, Wed 10am–10pm; train to Humlebæk, then by foot or bus no. 388) has become a superb platform for modern art from all over the world, and it continues to go from strength to strength.

ART IN THE LANDSCAPE

Although the gallery receives donations from other sources, Jensen allocated much of his fortune to the Louisiana foundation, and the state pays for some of the running costs.

Louisiana is no enclave for head-in-the-clouds artists. Its aim is to bring art to the whole of the community, irrespective of age and background. It is a work of art in itself, aiming to show the 'interplay between art, architecture and the landscape'. Several unusual museum buildings are spread out or across the site on the Øresund coast. The park consists of a harmonious array of mature shrubs, lines of reeds, neatly tended lawns and stately beeches, planes and pines with modern

Star Attractions
- **Karen Blixen Museet**
- **Louisiana Museum for Moderne Kunst**

Not just art...
The Louisiana Museum for Moderne Kunst at Humlebæk is a gallery with a difference. Set in beautiful gardens on the water's edge, it is easy to while away most of a day here soaking up the art and atmosphere. The café offers delicious Danish food, the shop has a wide selection of books, posters and designer items, and the Children's Wing runs a variety of inspired activities. Look out for any special exhibitions.

Dubuffet sculpture, the Louisiana Museum

Map on page 91

Hamlet's castle

Picturesque Helsingør, just 7km (4 miles) north along the coast from Louisiana, is the setting for ★★ **Kronborg**, Hamlet's 'Castle of Elsinore' (May–Sept: daily 10.30am–5pm; Oct–Apr: 11am–4pm, closed Mon; Nov–Mar: Tues–Sun 11am–3pm). This imposing Renaissance castle guarding the harbour was built to collect tolls for crossing the Sound. Visit the richly decorated King's and Queen's Chambers. The chapel and banqueting hall are also well worth seeing, and there is a maritime museum.

Frederiksborg Slot, interior

sculptures dotted amongst them, often occupying surprising but always visually pleasing locations. Art and landscape merge to create a natural atmosphere. With visitors relaxing on the grass or bathing in the lakes, it is easy to forget that this is a museum. Enjoy a picnic by a Moore, a Miró or an Arp and look across the Sound to Sweden.

A COLLECTION OF MASTERPIECES

The majority of the museum's treasures – mostly paintings, prints and sculptures – are kept in the two main buildings and in the pavilions, linked by airy promenades which help to bring nature closer. As the route changes, visitors find themselves below ground one minute and with panoramic views the next. Who knows what waits round the corner? It seems to lack order, and yet the surroundings subtly evoke the spirit of Picasso, Max Ernst, Asger Jorn and other CoBrA artists *(see page 104)*, Warhol, Rauschenberg, Calder, Giacometti and many others.

WEST TO FREDERIKSBORG SLOT

After Rosenborg Slot, ★★★ **Frederiksborg Slot** (open Apr–Oct: daily 10am–5pm; Nov–Mar: daily 11am–3pm) is probably the finest royal palace on Sjælland. Situated 35 km (22 miles) northwest of Copenhagen near **Hillerød**, it can be reached by S-train to Hillerød station, then bus no. 701 or 702.

At the start of the 17th century, Christian IV transformed his father's castle into a grand Renaissance-style castle, standing astride three tiny islands in Hillerød's town lake. The Dutch Renaissance, with its red bricks, bright sandstone and arching gables, is immortalised here. Some sections of the sandstone adornments were gilded and painted.

Frederik VII was the last monarch to reside at Frederiksborg. When a fire damaged the main block in 1859, he ordered it to be rebuilt, but restricted finances slowed down progress and, when Frederik died in 1863, work stopped completely. A begging bowl had to be rattled in front of some distinguished benefactors before the castle was saved from further decline.

NATIONAL HISTORY MUSEUM

Frederiksborg finally re-opened in 1884 as the Danish National History Museum, to be administered by the Carlsberg foundation. Now visitors can explore more than 70 magnificent rooms, including the Audience Room, the Knights' Hall, the Royal Wing, the Princes' Wing and the old church.

As well as paintings and royal portraits, many valuable pieces of furniture have found a fitting home in the castle.

ROSKILDE

According to legend, the Viking king Roar founded the town of Roskilde (pop. 50,000), about 30 km (19 miles) to the west of Copenhagen, on **Roskildefjord** around 600, making it one of Denmark's oldest towns. It was none other than the founder of Copenhagen, Bishop Absalon, who commissioned ★★★ **Roskilde Domkirke** (cathedral) in 1170 (open Apr–Sept: Mon–Fri 9am–4.45pm, Sat 9am–noon, Sun 12.30–4.45pm; Oct–Mar: Tues–Fri 10am–3.45pm

Below: Roskilde Domkirke, interior detail
Bottom: view of the cathedral

Map on page 91

and Sat and Sun 12.30–3.45pm as long as no church services are taking place; train to Roskilde or bus no. 6a or 123 from Copenhagen).

In the 13th century, the original Romanesque building was drastically altered to give the red-brick cathedral a French Gothic appearance. The distinctive spires were added in 1635.

Over the centuries, the cathedral was gradually extended to accommodate several burial chapels, the final resting places for a total of 38 kings and queens, some of whose sarcophagi are extravagantly decorated.

ELABORATE INTERIOR

A tour around the interior provides a lesson in Danish history. The first king to be buried here was Harald I (d. 985) and the last was Frederik IX (d. 1972). When furnishing the interior, only the best was good enough. Of particular note are the carved choir stalls (1420), the clock with the moving figures (*circa* 1500), the gilded high altar (late 16th century) and the remarkable bookstands in the chancel.

During the summer, the baroque Raphaelis organ (1554) is used for organ recitals. The Absalon arch, a relic from the first chapel (*circa* 1200) links the cathedral with the palace, formerly the **bishops' residence**.

Royal chapels

In Roskilde Cathedral, the chapel of King Christian IV, built in 1641 in Dutch Renaissance style with splendid murals, and that of King Frederik V, 1770, by the architect Harsdorff, are the most impressive and worth a look.

Admiring the gilded high altar

VIKING SHIP MUSEUM

In 1962 some extraordinary excavation work started in the Roskildefjord after archaeologists discovered the remains of several Viking ships. The ships were probably scuttled in the fjord between 1000 and 1050. It took a great deal of meticulous work first to remove the fragments from the mud and stones and then to conserve them.

The results of the laborious treatment can be seen in the ★★ **Vikingeskibsmuseet** (open daily 10am–5pm; train to Roskilde, then bus no. 607 or 216, or a 20-minute walk). There are five ships altogether, including an ocean-going merchant ship, a warship and an inshore boat which probably served as a ferry.

From the glass facade of the Viking Ship Museum it is possible to look out over the fjord, where reconstructions of Viking ships float on the water. During the summer they are used to take visitors for a trip on the fjord. Models, videos, special exhibitions, and a film showing how the boats were salvaged, form part of the museum.

SOUTH TO ARKEN'S MODERN ART

In order to boost the culturally barren southern environs of Copenhagen, ★★ **Arken Museet for Moderne Kunst** (open Tues–Sun 10am–5pm, Wed until 9pm; S-train to Ishøj station, then bus no. 128) was opened in 1996 in **Ishøj Strandpark** by the Baltic coast.

Nicknamed the 'Ark', this bold concrete design in the shape of a ship's hull, merges well with the surrounding countryside. The main art axis, which extends for the full length of the 'Ark', serves as the hub for all the other rooms. Concrete walls, some 12-metres (40-ft) high, and huge, riveted steel plates lend a harsh, uncompromising feel to the gallery, while the side rooms at various levels create a playful effect.

The bold and unusual design of the interior provides an ideal setting for the avant-garde works of art displayed here. As the museum's own collection is currently rather modest, special exhibitions are often the main focal point of a visit.

Star Attractions
- Vikingeskibsmuseet
- Arken Museet for
  Moderne Kunst

Below: Viking Ship on the Roskildefjord
Bottom: Arken Museet for Moderne Kunst

Art

Only after the Napoleonic War, when the people started to acquire a genuine sense of national identity, did Danish art begin to develop its own stylistic qualities. Previously, most artists, mainly painters and writers, had been swept along by central European currents, and patrons of the arts usually commissioned foreign artists and architects. The heyday of Danish art and culture is now referred to as the 'Golden Age' *(Guldalder)*.

PAINTING AND SCULPTURE

Copenhagen Art Academy, an institution founded in 1754, where most Danish painters and sculptors received their basic education, laid the foundations for the 'Golden Age'. The self-confidence of the artists who studied here was boosted by the fact that their academic mentor, the sculptor Bertel Thorvaldsen (1770–1844), had won international acclaim in Rome and was sought after by prestigious collectors from all over the world. Thorvaldsen now has his own museum in Copenhagen *(see page 42)*.

ECKERSBERG AND THE GOLDEN AGE

The painter, Christoffer Wilhelm Eckersberg (1783–1853) earned his first plaudits abroad. When he returned home in 1816 and became a professor at the Art Academy, the Royal Court commissioned him to paint historic paintings for the Christiansborg Palace. During his leisure time, he painted in the open air. These naturalistic works and Eckersberg's precise technique explain his special place in the Danish art world. In addition, he influenced a whole generation of young artists, who formed the 'hard core of the Golden Age' and included Christen Købke (1810–48), who concentrated on Danish themes and often painted in Copenhagen. It is interesting to compare the castle today with his paintings.

At the end of the 19th century the Skagen school of painters – named after the artists' colony

Best of the galleries
The most comprehensive collection of 19th- and 20th-century Danish art is to be found in Copenhagen's Statens Museum for Kunst, the Hirschsprungske Samling *(see page 54 for both)* and Ny Carlsberg Glyptotek *(see page 25)*. The Louisiana Museum for Moderne Kunst, to the north of Copenhagen *(see pages 97–98)*, has the finest collection of contemporary international art, while the younger generation of Danish artists display their works in the new Arken Museet for Moderne Kunst in Ishøj *(see page 101)*.

Opposite: detail of a Thorvaldsen sculpture
Below: Eckersberg's 'Morning Toilet' in the Hirschsprungske Samling

Artistic enlightenment
Although little known outside Denmark, the philosopher and theologian N.F.S. Grundtvig (1783–1872) had an enormous impact on the nation. He founded the folk high schools and promoted the teaching of art, music and history. Under his guidance, the peasantry became educated. Today's policy of generous state support for the arts is due in large part to the underlying egalitarian philosophy of this great 19th-century thinker.

in northern Jutland – turned their backs on the teachings of the Art Academy and became Denmark's principal exponents of Impressionism. Peter Severin Krøyer (1851–1909) and Anna Ancher (1859–1935) were the leading figures in the movement. Den Hirschsprungske Samling Museum (*see page 54*) contains a good cross-section of their work.

ART IN THE 20TH CENTURY

CoBrA (Copenhagen-Brussels-Amsterdam), an international group formed by the painter Asger Jorn (1914–73), disregarded academic tradition and devoted itself to abstract art. Jorn did not bother with preparatory sketches and painted spontaneously. But improvisation and experimentation were poorly received in Danish art circles, and in 1953 Jorn left the country.

During the 1960s, the private Experimental Art School came under the spotlight. Its most prominent member, the Copenhagen painter and sculptor Per Kirkeby (born 1938), started out as an experimental artist, joined the international art circle Fluxus and, during the 1970s, worked as a film producer. He has published a series of poetry books and has enjoyed a successful career as an architect. In 1987 he won the Thorvaldsen medal, the highest fine art award in the country.

Max Ernst sculpture at Louisiana

Literature

Denmark's first, internationally-recognised literary figure was Ludvig Holberg (1684–1754), a dramatist, lyricist and a professor at Copenhagen University. He produced a wealth of comedies, albeit with a serious message, and his work was performed at Denmark's first national theatre. He enjoyed great success with his Utopian story *Niels Klim's Underground Journey* (1741), in which he appointed himself as a spokesman for religious tolerance. Holberg wrote the novel in Latin, so that he could maximise his readership, but it was immediately translated into German, Dutch, French, English, Danish and Swedish, and ater into Russian and Hungarian. The book is still very popular and widely available today.

HANS CHRISTIAN ANDERSEN

Hans Christian Andersen (1805–75) gave folk tales a new, humorous twist. Between 1835 and 1875, he published no fewer than 150 fairytales with *Tin Soldier*, *The Ugly Duckling*, and *The Emperor's New Clothes* among the best known. Andersen came from a poor background and had to wait some time for recognition. He initially hoped for a career on the stage and only later did he discover his talent for writing. He lived in Copenhagen from 1819 onwards.

KIERKEGAARD AND BRANDES

The philosopher Søren Kierkegaard (1813–55) lived most of his life in Copenhagen. His literary works were unique, and he cannot be categorised under the usual aesthetic criteria as his writings consist of essays, philosophical analyses, polemics, literary criticism, psychological dissertations and religious theses. Kierkegaard is noted for his remarkable command of language, and also the complex structure of his works.

Georg Brandes (1842–1927) represents the transition from Romanticism to Naturalism. This

Below: Hans Christian Andersen
Bottom: fairytale set at the Tivoli

literary critic, essayist and (from 1902) professor at Copenhagen University expected the literature of the time to address contemporary problems, and wanted to bid farewell to Romantic idealism. Brandes influenced such writers as Jens Peter Jacobsen (1847–85), Herman Bang (1857–85) and the Norwegian Henrik Ibsen (1826–1906).

NEXØ'S EPIC

Martin Andersen Nexø (1869–1954) devoted himself to social criticism. His book *Pelle the Conqueror* (1906–10; 4 parts) describes poverty and exploitation among Danish peasants in the late 19th century. With its first-hand description, poverty as well as the growth of the labour movement, it was regarded by the socialist movement as a heroic epic. For a long time, however, Nexø was denied recognition by Danish literary circles.

Below: Karen Blixen photographed in 1931
Bottom: Gabriel Byrne and Julia Ormond in Smilla's Sense of Snow

THE NOVELS OF KAREN BLIXEN

Initially, Karen (Tania) Blixen (1885–1962) also had a difficult time in her native country. The greatest female writer in Danish literary history, she was a colourful personality with immense talent as a storyteller. Her 1938 novel *Out of Africa* provided the inspiration for a spectacular film in 1985 staring Meryl Streep and Robert Redford. Blixen's farmstead in Rungstedlund is now a museum *(see page 96)*.

MODERN LITERATURE

Contemporary Danish literature has fought bravely on the international book market, and has probably won proportionately more than its fair share. Pia Tafdrup, Inger Christensen, Henrik Stangerup and Klaus Rifbjerg are the established leaders, with Peter Høeg a name that has emerged in the 1990s. His subtle *Miss Smilla's Feeling for Snow* made quite an impact on Danish literature, and in 1997 *Smilla's Sense of Snow* became a Hollywood movie starring Julia Ormond, Gabriel Byrne and Vanessa Redgrave.

Music

Secular music was encouraged in the Royal Court during the 16th and 17th centuries. It maintained a choir of trained singers, an instrumental ensemble and a trumpet band. Christian IV (1588–1648) was the first king to bring renowned, foreign composers to Copenhagen, as highlighted in Rose Tremain's novel, *Music & Silence*, set in the Danish court. Extravagant dramatic works with music were staged, with ballet, orchestral music and, from 1689, opera, among the most popular productions.

Classical Viennese music, including the work of Haydn and Mozart, dominated the first third of the 19th century. Beethoven's compositions were only occasionally heard, usually on the initiative of Daniel Friedrich Rudolph Kuhlau (1786–1832), who wrote operas, and also the score for Johan Ludvig Heiberg's *Elverhøj*. He occupies a prominent place in the history of Danish music.

NIELSEN LEADS THE WAY

Carl August Nielsen (1865–1931) is another leading name. He not only wrote operas, symphonies, violin concertos and compositions for piano, but as the conductor of the Copenhagen Court Ensemble from 1907 to 1914 and then as director of the Copenhagen Conservatory, he also

Danish Royal Ballet
Ballet has a long established tradition in Denmark, and audiences regularly fill The Royal Theatre in Copenhagen for productions by the Royal Ballet (Aug–May). Under their great master, August Bournonville (1805–79), the company built up an international reputation for classical ballet. Contemporary choreography began to form an important part of the repertoire, under the inspired tuition of Harald Lander in the mid-20th century.

Concert-goers on Rådhuspladsen

Jazz Festival
Since the 1960s, Copenhagen has had a reputation for jazz, due in part to the brilliant American jazz saxophonist Ben Webster, who lived in the city. Jazz clubs and an annual jazz festival in early July continue the tradition. The calendar for rock and pop is equally lively, with concert venues and many pubs also providing a stage for established and up-and-coming groups *(see What's On, page 115).*

exerted a tremendous influence on Danish music.

Per Nørgård (born 1932) is the principal exponent of Danish avant-garde music, but Poul Ruders, Ib Nørholm, Pelle Gudmundsen-Holmgreen, Flemming Weis and Niels Viggo Bengtsson also deserve a mention.

Cinema

At the end of the 19th century, the new medium of moving pictures aroused considerable interest in Denmark. Copenhagen's first cinema, the 'Kosmorama' opened in 1904. Ole Olsen (1863–1943), one of the first cinema owners, invested a lot of money in the industry, and in 1906 he founded the 'Nordisk Films Kompagni', which is still in existence today and said to be the oldest film company in the world. He had a studio built, and employed the best producers and actors.

Olsen extended his empire into Germany and Russia, and up until World War I 'Nordisk' occupied a powerful position. By World War II, however, it had lost its markets outside Scandinavia as the best actors and actresses went abroad.

Emily Watson in Lars von Trier's Breaking the Waves

OSCAR-WINNING FILMS

In the 1980s Danish film-makers re-appeared on the international stage with works such as Gabriel Axel's *Babette's Feast* (1986) and Bille August's *Pelle the Conqueror* (1987); both of which won Oscars for Best Foreign Film.

Since then a new generation of Danish producers has been winning plaudits. In 1996, Lars von Trier was presented with an award at the Cannes Film Festival for his film, *Breaking The Waves*. Von Trier, among other Danish film-makers, including Thomas Vinterberg (*The Celebration*) and Søren Kragh-Jacobsen (*Mifune's Last Song*), is a signatory of the Dogme 95 Manifesto. This set of rules was designed as a challenge to reinvigorate film-making by moving away from the Hollywood genre in favour of true-life stories, shot on location using hand-held cameras, without the use of artificial lighting and sound.

Events Calendar

Most of Copenhagen's annual festivals involve music. For further details, contact the Tourist Office *(see page 121)*.

January: Venue Rock Festival, underground rock on the last weekend. At the usual rock venues.

Shrovetide: Beating the Barrel, carnival parade and *mardi gras* festivities, centred on Rådhuspladsen and the Nationalmuseet.

Whitsuntide: *Karneval i København*, carnival processions and concerts (rock, blues, folk and jazz). In the Fælledpark, Rosenborg Have and the inner city.

End of June: Roskilde Festival, the country's biggest rock festival. A long weekend in a country park Woodstock-style.

Beginning of July: Copenhagen Jazz Festival, with bands playing every jazz style from bebop onwards. On stage, in pubs and on the streets.

Mid-August–early September: *Glyptotekets Sommerkoncerter*, classical music in Ny Carlsberg Glyptotek.

September: 'Golden Days in Copenhagen' recalls the Golden Age with theatre, ballet and concerts, walking tours of the city and excursions. Full programme of events from the Tourist Office.

*Below: clowning around
Bottom: Harlequin and ballerina dance at the Tivoli*

FOOD AND DRINK

The Danes like to think of themselves as the 'French of the north'. Food and drink are important to their quality of life. They believe in 'living to eat' not 'eating to live'.

OPEN SANDWICHES

Visitors will soon come to appreciate that unique Danish creation, *smørrebrød* or 'bread and butter', but do not be misled by this over-simplification. Rye bread, thickly-spread with butter or goose lard, forms the basis for open sandwiches topped with salmon, eel, plaice, herring, beef, liver pâté, ham, steak tartare, egg, cheese, chicken breast, turkey or seafood, and then garnished with sauces and vegetables, salads and herbs. The usual time for a *smørrebrød* is mid-day, as a *frokost* or 'second breakfast'.

Copenhagen has several specialist *frokost* restaurants *(see page 113)* which are usually open from 10am to 5pm. Many *frokost* restaurants prepare the toppings, and the guest selects the type of bread, topping, sauce or marinade from the spread at the bar by marking a list; a pair of skilful hands will then make up the snack. There are also self-service counters, where you can buy a ready-made *smørrebrød* to take away.

DANISH CUISINE

The proper name for lunch is *middag*, although it's usually a family meal taken after 5pm. Danish cuisine comprises meat, often pork, plus potatoes and vegetables such as cabbage and leek. It should, however, not be assumed that Danes do not use rice, noodles or more exotic vegetables.

Left: smoked herring,
just one of many ways
of preparing this fish

There are plenty of good restaurants to choose from, and not all are expensive. Fish from the Øresund has only a modest reputation, so the restaurateurs have to procure it from further afield, and this partly explains why fish menus can be rather pricey. The Scandinavian buffet is also very popular. Guests can eat as much as they like from a range of displayed foods within a chosen price range.

PUB FOOD

If you want to eat well *and* cheaply, then go to one of the cafés, pubs or restaurants that serve hot meals at lunch-time. The choice of food will not be so great as in the evening, but it will be appetising and filling. The *dagens ret* (dish of the day), including coffee, is usually good value. Many newer cafés serve cheap snacks and light meals throughout the day. Copenhagen has many mobile snack bars, serving *pølser* (sausages) in a variety of ways.

> **Drinking**
> The drinking of aquavit *(schnapps)* and beer are both deeply rooted in Danish culture. *Schnapps* is a fiery brew distilled from potatoes and grain that is traditionally drunk ice cold with *smørrebrød*, or to round off a meal. It is flavoured with herbs and spices, including caraway seed, cumin, dill and fennel, and there are many different varieties to choose from.
>
> Beer *(øl)* drinking has been popular in Denmark since Viking times. Today there are 30 breweries producing around 150 varieties of differing strengths, either bottled or draught. Pilsener *(Tuborg grøn, Carlsberg Hof)* is the standard brew. Stronger ales include *Guld Tuborg* and *Carlsberg Elefant*. Lighter beers and alcohol-free brands are also available.

Restaurant selection

The following entries are recommended restaurants in Copenhagen, listed according to three categories: €€€ = expensive; €€ = moderate; € = inexpensive.

GOURMET RESTAURANTS

Alberto K at The Royal, Hammerichsgade 1, tel: 33 42 61 61. Mon–Sat 6–10.30pm. Gourmet restaurant (modern Italian based on Danish ingredients) on the 20th floor of Royal Hotel – across the street from Tivoli. Arne Jacobsen functionalism down to the smallest detail, ambitious food, and maybe the best view of the city – and there are windows all the way round on three sides of the restaurant. €€€.

Krogs Fiskerestaurant, Gammel Strand 38, tel: 33 15 89 15. Mon–Sat noon–3pm, and 6pm–10.30pm. This is a splendid fish restaurant with a lovely view over the Gammel Strand. Bouillabaisse, sole, eel, salmon and lobster served in a variety of ways. €€€.

Restaurationen, Møntergade 19, tel: 33 14 94 95. Tues–Sat 6pm–midnight. Restaurationen has received almost every star that magazine and food writers have to give, including the Michelin and Wine Spectator award of excellence. The menu is set every week, it is unique and chosen according to the season. The expertise of the cuisine and the welcoming atmosphere make it worth the high prices. €€€.

TyvenKokkenHansKoneogHendesElsker, Magstræde 16, tel: 33 16 12 92. Mon–Sat 6pm–2am. Very romantic. The speciality is a seven course menu, which is boldly composed and inspired by many cuisines. The dishes can for example be couscous with cardamom sauce or scallop with pear. The prices are above medium. €€€.

Viva, Langebro Kajplads 570 (by Langebro bridge), tel: 27 25 05 05. Mon–Sat 11.30am–3pm, 5.30–10pm; Sun 5.30–9pm. Dive into Viva's sea of creative hors d'ouvres aboard a stylish ship. Untraditionally, the evening menu consists only of hors d'ouvres from the sea. €€€.

DANISH DINERS

Bjælkehuset, Valby Langgade 2; tel 36 30 00 27. 11am–11pm. Closed in winter. A beautiful parkland setting

> 👁 **Danish pastries**
> Treat yourself to an authentic Danish pastry *(wienerbrød)* with your morning coffee, or a cream layered cake in the afternoon. Konditori La Glace, Skoubogade, off Strøget, offers a mouth-watering selection.

for a traditional Danish lunch. €€.

Bryggeriet Apollo, Vesterbrogade 3, tel: 33 12 33 13. Open Mon–Thurs 11.30am–1am, Fri and Sat till 2am, Sun 3pm–midnight. Dine between the copper beer kettles. Solid and good food and a new beer every month. €€.

Det Lille Apotek, Store Kannikestræde 15, tel: 33 12 56 06. Open Mon–Sat 11am–midnight, Sun noon–midnight. 'The Little Pharmacy' is the oldest cellar restaurant with antique furnishings. Popular with students. €€.

Peder Oxe, Gråbrødretorv 11, tel: 33 11 00 77. Open daily 11.30am–1am. Danish and French cuisine in a row of fine restaurants on this attractive square. Outdoor seating, great salad bar, good wine list. €€.

Tivoli: Grøften, (tel: 33 75 06 75), with its red and white check tablecloths, is a popular spot. Diners in the more stylish **Balkonen** (tel: 33 75 07 27) have a pleasant view. Both open daily, noon–midnight. Danish and French dishes. Both €€.

FROKOST RESTAURANTS

Café & Ølhalle 1892, Rømersgade 22, tel: 33 33 00 47. Open daily 11.30am–4pm. This 'Café and Beer Hall' is part of the Workers' Museum. Original turn-of-the-century atmosphere. Real Danish fare. **€**.

Caféen i Nikolaj, Nikolaj Plads 12, tel: 70 26 64 64. Mon–Sat 11.30am–5pm. In a wing of the Nikolaj Church, popular with the locals. Menus and *frokost*. **€–€€**.

Ida Davidsen, Store Kongensgade 70, tel: 33 91 36 55. Mon–Fri 10am–4pm. Family-run concern in Frederiksstaden serving a delectable spread of *smørrebrød*. Traditional decor. **€–€€**.

Kanal-Kaféen, Frederiksholms Kanal 18, tel: 33 11 57 70. Mon–Fri 11.30am–7pm, Sat 10.30am–4pm. Enjoy a *smørrebrød* in a maritime atmosphere at this café. Herring from the fishing grounds off Bornholm. **€**.

Kongens Kælder, Gothersgade 87, tel: 33 12 87 19. Mon–Sat 11am–4pm. Pure *frokost*. Take a list and tick what you want. **€**.

Sorgenfri, Brolæggerstræde 8, tel: 33 11 58 80. Daily 10am–11pm. Central location, serving *smørrebrød* below ground level. Good reputation. **€**.

INTERNATIONAL CUISINE

Ankara, Vesterbrogade 35, tel: 33 31 92 33. Open daily noon–midnight. Popular Turkish buffet. **€–€€**.

Indian Taj, Jernbanegade 3–5, tel: 33 13 10 10. Daily noon–11.30pm. Scandinavia's first Indian restaurant. Good value. Traditional decor. **€€**.

Mongolian Barbecue, Stormgade 35, tel: 33 14 64 66. Open daily 4pm–midnight. An interesting alternative; situated at the rear of the National Museum. **€€**.

San Giorgio, Rosenborggade 7 (near the Kultorvet), tel: 33 12 61 20. Open daily 5pm–midnight. Authentic pizza and pasta dishes. **€€–€€€**.

Shezan, Viktoriagade 22, tel: 33 24 78 88. Daily 11.30am–11.30pm. Pakistani specialities. **€€**.

Thai Esan1, Lille Istedgade 7, tel: 33 24 98 54. Open Sun–Thur noon–11pm, Fri–Sat noon–midnight. Authentic, carefully prepared Thai food. **€–€€**.

VEGETARIAN

Den Grønne Kælder, Pilestræde 48, tel: 33 93 01 40. Mon–Sat 11am–10pm. Excellent vegetarian lunch. **€–€€**.

Café Society

Bang & Jensen, Istedgade 35, tel: 33 25 53 18. Mon–Fri 8am–2am, Sat 10am–2am, Sun 10am–midnight. Trendy café in the lively part of Istedgade. Late brunch, Saturday night cocktail bar.

Café Klaptræet, Kultorvet 11, tel: 33 13 40 38. Mon–Wed 10am–1am, Thurs 10am–3am, Fri 10am–5am, Sat 11am–5am, Sun 11am–midnight. Film posters and spotlights remain from its days as a cinema. Popular with young people.

Café Norden, Østergade 61, tel: 33 11 77 91. Open daily 9am–midnight, Sun opens 10am. Classic café atmosphere in typical Art Nouveau style.

Café Sommersko, Kronprinsensgade 6, tel: 33 14 81 89. Mon–Wed 8am–midnight, Thurs 8am–1am, Fri 8am–4am, Sat 9am–4am, Sun 10am–midnight. The forerunner of the Copenhagen modern café scene. The red sofas add a touch of panache.

Café Wilder, Wildersgade 56, on the corner of Skt Annæ Gade, tel: 31 54 71 83. Mon 9am–midnight, Tues and Wed 9am–1am, Thurs–Fri 9am–2am, Sat 9.30am–2am, Sun 9.30am–midnight. In Christianshavn. Youthful, casual atmosphere behind a glass facade.

Kafe Kys, Læderstræde 7, tel: 33 93 85 94, Sun–Thur 10am–1am, Fri–Sat 10am–2am. Attracts many young people. Outdoor serving in summer. Popular on Friday nights.

WHAT'S ON

Copenhagen's Tourist Office *(see pages 121)* keeps a wide selection of publications but, for the best 'what's on' guide, consult the monthly English-language magazine *Copenhagen This Week* (or the listings section of *The Copenhagen Post*). This handy journal contains additional information about advance ticket sales and exhibitions, has a practical A–Z guide and lists almost every café, pub and restaurant in the city. Note that the 'Late Night' section provides information on those places which serve food until late into the night; it is not a list of nightclubs. Tickets for concerts, plays, ballet, opera and other events can be obtained through **BilletNet** at Post Offices, tel: 70 15 65 65; website: www.billetnet.dk

THEATRE

Det Kongelige Teater (The Royal Theatre) by Kongens Nytorv, tel: 33 69 69 69, provides a home for drama and ballet. While plays in Danish may not have much appeal for foreign visitors, it is definitely worth enquiring

The Royal Theatre entrance

about tickets for ballet performances. Advance ticket sales Monday to Friday. Opera performances take place in Operaen at Holmen. One handy tip: from 5pm onwards, the Royal Theatre box office offers 50 percent reductions on unsold tickets for events taking place that day.
Det Ny Teater, Gammel Kongevej 29, tel: 33 25 50 75, stages hit musicals in Danish. Closed in the summer months.
Kanonhallen, Øster Fælled Torr 37, tel: 35 43 20 21, is a venue for international dance and theatre festivals, especially during the summer.

ROYAL BALLET COMPANY

The Copenhagen Royal Ballet Company has a particularly good reputation. Vicenzo Galeotti (1775–1816), August Bournonville (1833–77) and Harald Lander (balletmaster at the Royal Danish Ballet School from 1932 to 1951) were all innovative figures on the Danish ballet scene.

Lander engaged classical and avant-garde dancers and, in so doing, quickly enhanced the Royal Ballet's international reputation. The company performs at Det Kongelige Teater between late August and June.

OPERA

Operaen, Ekvipagemestervej 10, tel: 33 69 69 33. The Copenhagen Opera House hosts opera, classical and ballet performances in spectacular surroundings. For tickets tel: 33 69 69 69.

CLASSICAL MUSIC

Tivoli Koncertsalen, Vesterbrogade 3, tel: 33 15 10 12. The Concert Hall in the pleasure gardens is home to the Sjælland Symphony Orchestra, which accompanies singers, guest musicians and conductors. Foreign orchestras also perform here. There is a separate entrance on Tietgensgade 20. Some concerts are free of charge.

Concerts are also held at **Radiohusets Koncertsal**, Julius Thomsensgade 1, tel: 35 20 62 62.

CHURCH MUSIC

Concerts take place in Copenhagen's churches throughout the year and the vast majority of them are free – an admirable tradition. Ask in the Tourist Office for the concert programme, which is published every three or four months. Although it is written in Danish, the basic information will be perfectly understandable without any knowledge of the language.

ROCK AND BLUES

Loppen, Bådsmandsstræde 43, Christianshavn, tel: 32 57 84 22. One of the most popular venues. Huge beams, white walls and wooden floor in this old warehouse. Great relaxed atmosphere and music. Part of Christiania.
Mojo Blues Bar, Løngangsstræde 21C, tel: 33 11 64 53. Daily 8pm–5am. The leading blues scene in town. Situated between Rådhuspladsen and the National Museet.
Pumpehuset, Studiestræde 52, near Axeltorv, tel: 33 93 19 60. Daily 8pm–5am. This old waterworks (1859) is the top venue for rock music.

Stengade 30, Stengade 18, tel: 35 36 09 38. Danish and international rock and dance acts from the underground and the bubbling names followed by an all-night club. Nørrebro district.
Vega, Enghavevej 40, Vesterbro, tel: 33 25 70 11. Great 50's architecture is the frame for the two stages here. Varied musical programme. Vega Night Club is the stylish place for Friday and Saturday nights cum lounge. Ideal Bar (Wednesday to Saturday) is a relaxed bar with good music. Vega is truly the house of music in town.

OPEN-AIR CONCERTS

During the summer months, **Fælledpark**, north of the city centre in the Østerbro district, is often used for open-air concerts (from soul to country music).

DANCING

Rust, Guldbergsgade 8, tel: 35 24 52 00. Wednesday to Saturday 9pm–5am. Late night disco with café and bar. Three different bars to choose from. An intimate place with a lively atmosphere.
Club Mambo, Vester Voldgade 85, close to the City Hall, tel: 33 11 97 66. Open Thursday 9pm–2am Friday to

Jazz Clubs
Copenhagen JazzHouse, Niels Hemmingsensgade, tel: 33 93 26 16. Open for concerts 6pm–midnight, disco Thursday to Saturday, midnight–5am. As the city's top venue, this club attracts talent from throughout Denmark and beyond. Prime location in the city-centre.
La Fontaine, Kompagnistræde 11, paralell to Strøget, tel: 33 11 60 98. Open daily 8pm–5am. Legendary and intimate. Often unannounced jamsessions in late night.
Studenterhuset, Købmagergade 52, tel: 35 32 38 61. Live jazz on Thursdays in the Students' House. Relaxed student atmosphere.

Saturday 9pm–5am. Great place for salsa and other Latin American dancing. Popular with the very good dancers and latinos in town.

Woodstock, Vestergade 12, by Axeltorv, tel: 33 11 20 71. Thursday to Saturday 10pm–5am. '60s and '70s music not just for oldies.

Park Cafe & Nightclub, Østerbrogade 79, tel: 35 42 62 48. Cafe opens at noon. Nightclub opens at 11pm. Established disco in Østerbro. Revamped in '70s style.

GAY SCENE
Pan Disco, Knabrostræde 3, tel: 33 11 37 84. Popular three-storey venue.

LATE NIGHT SNACKS
Pasta Basta, Valkendorffsgade 22, tel: 33 11 21 31. Sunday to Thursday 11.30am–3am, Friday and Saturday 11.30am–5am. Pasta buffets and delicious salads – even after midnight. Reasonable prices. Central location.

RED LIGHTS
Copenhagen's lurid reputation as a sex metropolis began in 1969, when Denmark lifted its previous ban on pornography. Many of the sex shops that opened at the time to satisfy the mainly foreign visitors have now closed. However, Copenhagen still beats Hamburg or Amsterdam as the sex capital of Europe and the seamier side of the city is best avoided by visitors.

Internet Cafés
3D Net Café, Kattesundet 14, tel: 33 13 42 33. Open noon–midnight.
Boomtown, Axeltorv 1, opposite Tivoli, tel: 33 32 10 32. State of the art internet café. Open around the clock.
Nethulen, Istedgade 114, in Vesterbro, tel: 33 24 04 07. Open Monday to Friday 9.30am–11pm, Saturday to Sunday 4–11pm.

FUNFAIRS
Tivoli, Vesterbrogade 3 *(see page 22)* is not just a fairground and park, it also provides a stage for symphony concerts, jazz, pop, variety artists and pantomime.

Bakken, Dyrehavsbakken, Klampenborg *(see page 94)*. Occupying a part of the former royal hunting grounds of Klampenborg, less than 30 minutes' drive to the north of the city, this amusement park is more down-to-earth than the sophisticated Tivoli. There are a variety of rides and stalls on offer. Pieter Lieps' rustic restaurant in the forest is where the locals go for a romantic summer rendezvous.

CHILDREN'S ENTERTAINMENT
Zoo København, Roskildevej 32, tel: 72 20 02 00 *(see Route 8, page 85)*. Situated in Frederiksberg, this is a very popular destination for family days out. Apart from the usual attractions of lions, giraffes and seals, there is a Monkey House, Night Zoo and Children's Zoo.

Experimentarium, Tuborg Havnevej 7, tel: 39 27 33 33 *(see page 92)* in the northern district of Hellerup. The collection of hands-on activities, illustrating the wonders of science, attract children's attention. There is also the diverting Kid's Pavilion for 3–6 year olds.

Danmark's Akvarium, Kavalergården 1, tel: 39 62 32 83, in Charlottenlund *(see page 93)*. A fascinating insight into the colourful world of sea creatures.

Museums and galleries are not the fusty places they once were and Copenhagen's have gone out of their way to engage the interest of children, notably **Statens Museum for Kunst** *(see page 54)*, and **Louisiana Museum for Moderne Kunst** *(see page 97)*.

SHOPPING

SHOPPING STREETS

Linking Rådhuspladsen with Kongens Nytorv, the city's main shopping area takes in five streets and squares. Frederiksberggade, Nygade, Vimmelskaftet, Amagertorv and Østergade are known collectively as **Strøget**, or the 'Strip' *(see page 45).*

Starting from Rådhuspladsen, international fashion predominates with major outlets such as H&M and Esprit. Stately Royal Copenhagen, Georg Jensen and the design emporium Illums Bolighus overlook Amagertorv. Continuing towards Kongens Nytorv, designer names such as Prada, Kenzo, Louis Vuitton and Hermès can be found.

For individuality, make a detour into the maze of narrow streets either side of Strøget. Around **Fiolstræde**, for instance, which branches off near the Vimmelskaftet, is the university quarter, with a number of antiquarian bookshops. In **Kronprinsensgade** up and coming Danish designers such as Bruuns Bazaar, Munthe plus Simonsen, and Stig P, have their outlets. The little streets around **Larsbjørnsstræde** offer an eclectic mix of fashion, secondhand goods, and underground record shops. **Strædet** is for specialist shops selling items like glass and antique toys. Chic shoe shops and boutiques cluster aroung **Grønnegade**. For up-to-the-minute fashion, the boutiques in the **Scala Building** by Axeltorv offer a wide selection.

DEPARTMENT STORES

Magasin du Nord, Kongens Nytorv 13. A shoppers' paradise behind a Renaissance facade. Usually known simply as the 'Magasin'.

Illum, Østergade 52. The second-largest department store giant, with a reputation for quality. Antiques market on the second floor, plus a good restaurant on the roof terrace.

ANTIQUES AND RETRO

Quality antiques shops are concentrated mainly in the **Bredgade**, **Store Kongensgade**, **Kompagnistræde**, **Farvergade** and **Læderstræde** areas.

For shops specialising in retro clothes and memorablilia from the 1950s to the 1970s have a look around **Ravnsborgade** in Nørrebro and **Nordre Frihavnsgade** in Østerbro.

FLEA MARKETS

Loppemarked takes place from May to September. For a current list of markets, see the monthly publication *Copenhagen This Week*. Those listed below are held on a regular basis.

Gammel Strand. Saturday and Sunday, 8am–2pm. Includes good-quality antiques.

Israel Plads. Saturday, 8am–2pm. Typical flea market.

Frederiksberg, Smallegade. Saturday, 8am–2pm. In the square behind Frederiksberg Town Hall.

> **Danish Design**
> **Illums Bolighus**, Amagertorv 10. A furnishing company with its finger on the pulse of the latest in design and fashion.
> **Georg Jensen**, Amagertorv 4. Internationally renowned silversmith since 1904. Classic jewellery, cutlery and chandeliers.
> **Royal Copenhagen**, Amagertorv 6. Porcelain, glass and ornaments.
> **Holmegaard**, Østergade 15. Fine glassware from this southern Sjælland manufacturer.
> **Bang & Olufsen**, Kongens Nytorv 26. Hi-fi equipment with visual appeal. Worth a visit, even if only to browse.

PRACTICAL INFORMATION

Getting There

BY PLANE

Copenhagen airport is situated to the east of the town on Amager Island. A rail shuttle service links Kastrup and Copenhagen's central station; journey time about 12 minutes.

> **Flight Information**
> The following airlines serve Copenhagen from the UK:
> **Scandinavian Airlines (SAS)**, tel: 0870 60 727 727, www.scandinavian.net; **Sterling**, tel: 0870 787 8038, www.sterling.dk; **British Airways**, tel: 0870 850 9850, www.british airways.com; **British Midland**, tel: 0870 6070 555, www.flybmi.com; **EasyJet**, tel: 0871 244 2366, www.easyjet.com

BY TRAIN

Trains arrive daily from Germany, Britain and Sweden. Hovedbanegården, the central station, is situated opposite Tivoli and the Tourist Office. Buses for onward journeys leave either from outside the station or the nearby Rådhuspladsen. The S-trains leaving from the central station run on a separate network. For information on trains from the UK, tel **Rail Europe**: 08708 371 371; www.raileurope.co.uk; or via **DFDS Seaways**, tel: 08702 520 524; www.dfds.co.uk

BY BUS

For information on coach travel to Denmark, contact **Eurolines**, tel: 08705 143 219 or 08705 808 080; website: www.eurolines.com. The buses stop at Copenhagen's central station.

BY BOAT

Copenhagen is easily accessible by sea. The main ferry crossings to Denmark from Germany are Puttgarden and Rødby, Kiel and Bagenkop, Travemünde and Gedser. There are also numerous services from Norway and Sweden, and the Øresund bridge links Malmö with Copenhagen. **DFDS Seaways**, tel: 08702 520 524, operate ferries to Esbjerg on Denmark's west coast from Harwich. During the summer months, Esbjerg can also be reached by car ferry from Newcastle. It's advisable to book well in advance.

BY CAR

Most British visitors to Denmark arrive either by ferry direct from the UK or from Germany, and then either on the motorway from Hamburg in the west, or by car ferry across the Femer Bælt from Puttgarden to Rødby.

The E47, covers the last 165km (102 miles) to Copenhagen. Boats leave Puttgarden throughout the day every half hour and the journey takes just under an hour. You don't normally have to wait very long, except on busy summer weekends. Traffic can also be heavy at these times on the main road border crossing north of Flensburg.

Both the Storebælt bridge/tunnel from Funen to Sjælland, and the Øresund bridge from Malmö to Copenhagen levy a toll.

Getting Around

BY CAR

In Denmark, drive on the right-hand side of the road. Take with you a UK or EU driving licence and a warning triangle, and wear a seat belt at all times. Speed limits are 110 or 130 kph (66 or 80 mph) on motorways, 80 kph (46 mph) on other roads and 50 kph (30 mph) in a built-up area. Car hire companies operating in Denmark include: **Europcar**, tel: 0845 758

5375, www.europcar.com and **Hertz**, tel: 08708 44 88 44, www.hertz.co.uk

Parking

There are four different colour-coded zones within Greater Copenhagen; the closer to the city centre, the higher the charges. In the red zone, the most expensive, the maximum stay is 10 hours. Obtain a parking slip from a ticket machine. Charges in the red and green zones apply on weekdays from 8am to 10pm, and on Saturday from 8am to 5pm.

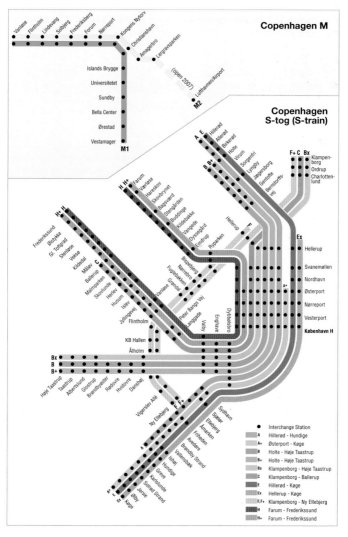

Copenhagen M

Copenhagen S-tog (S-train)

●	Interchange Station
A	Hillerød – Hundige
A+	Østerport – Køge
B	Holte – Høje Taastrup
B+	Holte – Høje Taastrup
Bx	Klampenborg – Høje Taastrup
C	Klampenborg – Ballerup
E	Hillerød – Køge
Ex	Hellerup – Køge
F,F+	Klampenborg – Ny Ellebjerg
H	Farum – Frederikssund
H+	Farum – Frederikssund

BY BUS

The bus network covers practically every destination and must be the best way to get around. Nearly all buses stop at either Rådhuspladsen or the Central Station. Passengers enter at the front and alight at the rear. The urban area is divided into zones and the pricing system is rather complicated, so just tell the driver where you want to go. The Copenhagen Card *(see below)* or a period ticket, valid for one day, can be used in every zone. Show your ticket when entering the bus.

BY S-TRAIN

The S-train connects Copenhagen and other towns on Sjælland. Within the city, it runs underground. Tickets are available at all S-stations.

BY METRO

The metro was inaugurated in 2002 and consists of just 2 lines. It connects with the S-train at Nørreport Station and with buses as well. You can use the same ticket as for the bus and S-train.

BY BICYCLE

Cyclists enjoy equal status with motorists on Copenhagen's roads, and consequently they usually make rapid and relatively safe progress. When using the cycleways, keep to the right.

If you don't have your own bike, use one of the **City Bikes**. You will see these sturdy two-wheelers at 110 sites around the city between April and November. They can be released with a 20-krone coin. You get your money back when you return the bike to any one of the racks. Pick up a **City Bike Map** from the Tourist Information Office *(see page 121)*. For addresses of bike hire companies, look in *Copenhagen This Week*.

THE COPENHAGEN CARD

The Copenhagen Card grants free admission to almost all museums, castles and many other sights, free travel on city buses, metro and S-trains and reductions on certain sightseeing trips. It can be bought to last for 24 hours or 72 hours. When you purchase the card, it is stamped with the starting date and the user enters the time it is first used. You also receive a comprehensive booklet with details of opening times, transport and a map.

The card may be purchased from the Tourist Office, at most hotels, travel agents, stations and at the airport.

Enjoying a day out in Nyhavn

Facts for the Visitor

TRAVEL DOCUMENTS

Most visitors – including citizens of the UK, USA, Canada, Eire, Australia and New Zealand – need only a passport, which is valid for at least three months at the time of entry.

CUSTOMS

When travelling to Denmark from the UK, the following may be taken into the country: 1.5 litres alcohol and 300 cigarettes or 75g cigars or 400g tobacco. Wine, beer and perfume can be brought in without restriction as long as they are for personal use.

Since the abolition of the duty-free system within the European Union, if you are an EU visitor you may buy as much as you like during your journey, provided it is for your own use.

'Duty free' is still available for visitors travelling from outside the EU.

TOURIST INFORMATION ABROAD

When planning your holiday, contact the Danish Tourist Board, which will supply leaflets and brochures.

In the UK: Danish Tourist Board, 55 Sloane Street, London SW1X 9SY, tel: 020 7259 5959; www.visitdenmark.com.
In Ireland: Royal Danish Embassy, 121–122 St Stephen's Green, Dublin 2; tel: 01 475 6404; www.ambdublin.um.dk.
In the US: The Danish Tourist Board, 655 Third Avenue, 18th floor, New York, NY 10017, tel: 212 885 9700; Scandinavian Tourist Board, 150 North Michigan Avenue, Suite 2110, Chicago, IL 60601, tel: 312 726 1120; Scandinavian Tourist Board, 8929 Wiltshire Boulevard, Beverly Hills, CA 90211, tel: 213 854 1549.

IN DENMARK

Information in Copenhagen is available from Wonderful Copenhagen's new tourist centre: Copenhagen Right Now, Vesterbrogade 4A, just opposite the main entrance of Tivoli, tel: 70 22 24 42; e-mail: touristinfo@woco.dk; website: www.visitcopenhagen.dk.

The following are provided free of charge: city map, what's on guide, information on sightseeing, transport, dining out, obtaining English-speaking guides and reservation of concert and theatre tickets. Hotel reservations *(see page 124)* are arranged for a small fee. Open September to April, Mon–Fri 9am–4pm, Sat 9am– 2pm; May and June, Mon–Sat 9am–6pm, July and August Mon–Sat 9am–8pm, Sun 10am–5pm.

Use It, Youth Tourist Information Centre, Rådhusstræde 13, 1466 København K, tel: 33 73 06 20; www.useit.dk (mid-June to mid Sept, daily 9am–7pm, mid-Sept to mid-June Mon–Wed 11am–4pm, Thurs till 6pm, Fri till 2pm), is a meeting place for young people, which provides information on budget accommodation and restaurants, sightseeing excursions, events and lifts.

> **Copenhagen Websites**
> **www.visitcopenhagen.dk** is the city's official website and contains useful information about where to stay, eating out, where to shop and festivals. Other helpful sites include www.copenhagentourism.net and www.aok.dk, which contains listings of restaurants, accommodation and entertainment.

CURRENCY

The *krone* (DKK) is the Danish currency. 1 *krone* = 100 *øre*. You will find notes to the value of 50, 100, 200, 500 and 1,000 *kroner*, coins at 1, 2, 5, 10 and 20 *kroner*, plus 25 and 50 *øre*, but *øre* are usually rounded up or down. Most banks have 24-hour teller machines (ATM) – look for the word *Kontanten* – and you can draw out up to 3,000DKK with some credit cards, but expect to pay a commission whether you use the machine or cash a cheque at the counter. Well-known traveller's cheques can be cashed in banks and at many hotels, restaurants and shops. There are no restrictions on importing and exporting currencies.

SIGHTSEEING TOURS
City walks
Two-hour guided tours of the central area with English-speaking guide. Meet in the Tourist Office. 1 May to 30 September at 10.30am.

Bus tours
Start in Rådhuspladsen in front of the Palace Hotel, tel: 32 66 00 00. Children half-price. Short tours: duration: 1hr 30 mins. 15 May to 15 June, daily at 9.30am and 3pm; 1 June to 15 September, daily at 9.30am, 1pm, and 3pm.

City and harbour tours (part of tour by boat): duration 2hrs 30 mins. 15 May to 15 June, daily at 9.30am; 16 June to 15 September, daily at 9.30am, 1pm and 3pm. Copenhagen Excursions, tel: 32 66 00 00. This tour can be booked at the Tourist Information Office *(see page 121).*

Grand tour of Copenhagen with visit to Langelinie, Gefion Fountain and Amalienborg: duration: 2hrs 30 mins. 1 April to 30 September, daily at 11am and 1.30pm; otherwise daily at 11am, Sunday at 1.30pm. Auto Paaske, tel: 32 66 00 00.

Castle Tour of North Sjælland, including Hamlet's castle of Kronberg, the Queen's summer residence of Fredensborg, and Frederiksborg Castle with the National Historical Museum. Duration: 7 hrs. 1 May to 15 October, Wednesday, Saturday and Sunday at 10.15am; otherwise Wednesday and Sunday at 10.15am. Price of lunch not included. Auto Paaske, tel: 32 66 00 00.

Harbour and canal tours
Canal tours: duration: 1 hr. Leave from Gammel Strand, Nyhavn, Little Mermaid. Beginning of April until end of September, daily 10am–5pm; 20 June to 10 August, until 7.30pm. Departures every half hour with multi-lingual commentary. Canal Tours, tel: 33 96 30 00.

Water bus: duration: 1 hr. Leave from Gammel Strand, Nyhavn. Little Mermaid. 1 May to 30 September, daily 10.15am–4.45pm. Departures every half hour. No guide. 1 June to 31 August, from the Little Mermaid to Trekronor Fortress in the Øresund; supplement payable.

TELEPHONE
Coin- and card-operated telephone kiosks can be found all over the city, but most are open to the elements and it's not always easy to carry on a normal conversation. 1, 2, 5, 10 and 20DKK coins, and cards to the value of 30, 50 and 100DKK are accepted. The latter may be bought from post offices and pavement kiosks.

To phone the UK, dial 0044 followed by the telephone number, omitting the first zero. Eight-digit numbers (without codes) apply throughout

---

👁 Opening Times
Opening times in Denmark are not strictly regulated and the following should be regarded only as guidelines. Many shops on Strøget are open on Sundays.
Banks: Monday–Friday 9.30am–4pm or 5pm; bureau de change until 10pm.
Post offices: Monday to Friday 9/10am–5/6pm, Saturday 9am–noon.
Shops: Monday to Wednesday 9/10am–5.30/6pm, Thursday, Friday until 7/8pm, Saturday until noon, though many shops in the city remain open until 5pm.

Denmark. To call Denmark from abroad, dial 0045 followed by the telephone number. Access codes for American visitors are as follows: MCI 8001 0022; Sprint 800 10 877; AT&T 8001 0010.

MEDICAL

Citizens of EU countries are entitled to free medical treatment in Danish hospitals on production of the E111 document. For minor complaints, however, patients pay the doctor or dentist at the time of treatment and then claim the fees back from the local health service offices.

The staff at the Tourist Information Office will provide the address and also offer guidance on the choice of doctor. It is nevertheless advisable to take out a private medical and accident insurance policy to cover all eventualities.

Medicines are available from chemists *(apotek)*, and a prescription is not always necessary. Steno Apotek, Vesterbrogade 6C, tel: 33 14 82 66, provides a 24-hour service.

DISABLED

Public buildings such as post offices, museums, art galleries and hotels normally provide reasonable facilities for the disabled. A booklet available from the Danish Tourist Board *(see page 121)* offers useful information for disabled users of public transport, hotels, restaurants and tourist attractions.

Holiday Care offers advice and services to disabled travellers and their families, www.holidaycare.org.uk; tel: 01293 774535.

In Denmark itself, contact The Danish Council of Organisations of Disabled People, Kløverprisvej 10 B, st., DK-2650 Hvidovre; tel: 36 75 17 77; fax: 36 75 14 03; e-mail: dsi@handicap.dk; website: www.handicap.dk

EMERGENCIES

For police, fire-brigade and ambulance, dial 112. This call is free from telephone boxes.

LOST AND FOUND

Police at Slotsherrensvej 113, Vanløse, tel: 38 74 88 22. Monday, Wednesday and Friday 9am–2pm, Tuesday and Thursday 9am–5.30pm.

TIPPING

Restaurant bills include a service charge, but many customers reward good service with a cash tip. Taxi drivers do not regard a tip as essential since tips are included in the fare but will welcome any extra.

DIPLOMATIC REPRESENTATION

British Embassy, Kastelsvej 36–40, 2100 Copenhagen Ø, tel: 35 44 52 00. **US Embassy**, Dag Hammerskjölds Allé 24, 2100 Copenhagen Ø, tel: 35 55 31 44.

TIME ZONE

Denmark is one hour ahead of GMT. Danish Summer Time begins on the last Sunday in March, when clocks go forward one hour, and ends on the last Sunday in October.

NEWS IN ENGLISH

To hear the news in English, tune into MW 1062 kHz, Monday to Friday 10.30am, 5.10pm and 10pm.

Public Holidays
Banks, offices and most shops close on New Year's Day, Maundy Thursday, Good Friday, Easter Sunday, Easter Monday, May Day, Great Prayer Day (*Store Bededag*, on the fourth Friday after Easter), Ascension Day, Whit Sunday, Whit Monday, Constitution Day (5 June), Christmas Day, Boxing Day, New Year's Eve.

ACCOMMODATION

When you are looking around for accommodation, a number of factors have to be weighed up. A centrally-located hotel can save time and money when visiting the main sights, and the public transport system is very efficient.

On the other hand, the city-centre hotels do not usually have car parks, and those a few stops from the centre are sometimes less expensive.

Generally speaking, it is better to use the Wonderful Copenhagen room-finding service offered by the Tourist Office *(see box)*. You state your requirements and the computer finds a suitable room. If you are visiting the city out of season, you can often save money as hotels reduce rates to fill their rooms.

Many of the larger hotels that have facilities for conferences and meetings make reductions at the weekend or during the holiday season. Breakfast is included in the published price, unless otherwise stated.

A free copy of the *Guide – Hotels, Inns & Holiday Centres* is available

from the Danish Tourist Board, and listings are published on the website www.danishhotels.dk

To book hotel accommodation contact: **Wonderful Copenhagen Hotel Booking**, tel: 45-70 22 24 42; e-mail: www.visitcopenhagen.dk; open Mon to Fri 9am–4pm. **Easybook**, tel: 45-35 38 00 37; fax: 45-35 38 06 37 (open Mon to Fri 9am–6pm, Sat 9am–2pm). Bed & breakfast accommodation can be booked through the Tourist Office *(see page 121)*. You should check whether breakfast is included in the price.

HOTEL SELECTION
The following selection of Copenhagen hotels are divided into three categories: €€€ = expensive; €€ = moderate; € = inexpensive.

€€€
Hotel d'Angleterre, Kongens Nytorv 34, 1050 Copenhagen K, tel: 33 12 00 95; fax: 33 12 11 18 www.remmen.dk The wealthy, the important and the beautiful take refuge behind the grand facade on Kongens Nytorv. Elegant rooms with a rather stiff, old-fashioned atmosphere.

Camping in style

Copenhagen Admiral Hotel, Toldbodgade 24–28, 1253 Copenhagen K, tel: 33 74 14 14; e-mail: booking@admiralhotel.dk; Two warehouses from the 1780s have been restored to create this waterside hotel. Exposed beams and fine view over the Øresund. www.admiralhotel.dk

71 Nyhavn Hotel, Nyhavn 71, 1051 Copenhagen K, tel: 33 43 62 00; fax: 33 43 62 01; e-mail: 71nyhavnhotel@arp-hansen.dk. Expensively renovated warehouse situated by the waterside with a great view of Nyhavn, Sund and the ferry terminal. www.71Nyhavnhotel.dk

€€

Bertrams Hotel, Vesterbrogade 107, 1602 Copenhagen V, tel: 33 25 04 05; fax: 33 25 04 02 e-mail bertrams@hotelguldsmeden.dk. On the main street through Vesterbro. Intimate hotel with friendly rooms and possibly Copenhagen's narrowest lift. www.hotelguldsmeden.dk

Hotel Christian IV, Dronningens Tværgade 45, 1302 Copenhagen K, tel: 33 32 10 44; fax: 33 32 07 06. Centrally located near Rosenborg Have. Pleasant atmosphere. Quiet rooms with window overlooking courtyard. www.hotelchristianiv.dk

Hotel Cosmopole, Colbjørnsensgade 5–11, 1652 Copenhagen V, tel: 33 21 33 33; fax: 33 31 33 99; e-mail cosmopol@pip.dknet.dk. Noisy nightclubs for neighbours, but, situated near station, it has the best location in this category. Some spacious rooms.

Hotel Esplanaden, Bredgade 78, 1260 Copenhagen K, tel: 33 48 10 00; fax: 33 48 10 66; e-mail co.esplanaden@choice.dk. Bright, high-ceilinged rooms behind an impressive, classical facade. The choice of furnishings was apparently based on a survey carried out among guests.

Hotel Fox, Jarmers Plads 3, 1551 Copenhagen V, tel: 33 13 30 00; fax:

33 14 30 33. By the busy Ørstedsparken. Only 10-minute walk to Rådhuspladsen. Trendy hotel with large rooms, individually decorated by 21 international artists. Ipods available to rent. www.hotelfox.dk

Front, Skt Annæ Plads 21,1250 Copenhagen K, tel: 33 13 34 00; fax: 33 11 77 07. Stylish hotel a short distance from the quay at Nyhavn. Some rooms have a harbour view. Quiet location. www.front.dk

€

Hotel Cab Inn City, Mitchellsgade 14, 1568 Copenhagen, tel: 33 46 16 16; e-mail: city@cabinn.dk. Unusual rooms rather like ferry cabins. Right in the city centre. Located 100 metres (330 ft) from Tivoli Gardens and 400 metres (1,310 ft) from the City Hall. www.cab-inn.dk

Hotel Fy & Bi, Valby Langgade 62, 2500 Valby, tel: 36 45 44 00; fax: 36 45 44 09. A charming 100-year-old building painted in traditional Danish yellow, offering modern facilities, a good restaurant and an excellent Danish breakfast buffet. A few minutes' walk from the Zoo and just 10 minutes by bus or S-train from the city centre. www.hotelfyogbi.dk

Top Hotel Hebron, Helgolandsgade 4, 1653 Copenhagen V, tel: 33 31 69 06; fax: 33 31 90 67. Close to the Central Railway Station and Tivoli, and convenient for the shops of Strøget. www.hebron.dk

---

Castles and Manor Houses

A number of Denmark's historic castles and manor houses have been converted into attractive hotels, often with excellent restaurants, and some in Sjælland are within easy reach of the capital. For details contact Danske Slotte & Herregaarde, Frederiksberggade 2, 1.th., 1459 Copenhagen K, tel: 86 60 38 44; www.slotte-herregaarde.dk.

INNS

Inns offer a characterful alternative to larger hotels. Inn cheques, which offer a discount on room rates, are available from tourist offices. Contact Danske Kroferie & Hoteller, tel: 45-75 64 87 00; fax: 45-75 64 87 20; e-mail: info@krohotel.dk; www.kro hotel.dk

YOUTH HOSTELS

Danish youth hostels generally offer a good standard of accommodation and welcome people of all ages, including children. The Tourist Board issues a list of *Youth & Family Hostels*, and further details appear on: www.danhostel.dk

To book accommodation you will need to be a holder of a valid Youth Hostel Association membership card. Contact the Youth Hostels Association for England and Wales, tel: 01629 592600; Scotland, 01786 891 400; Northern Ireland, 02890 32 47 33. The International Youth Hostel card can be bought from the hostel on arrival.

Copenhagen Danhostel Amager, Vejlandsallé 200, 2300 Copenhagen S, tel: 32 52 29 08; fax: 32 52 27 08. 2 January to 15 December. 512 beds. The most modern of the youth hostels around the city. Situated in a thinly-populated corner of Amager Island, reached by bus nos. 46 or 37, then 16.

Copenhagen Danhostel Bellahøj, Herbergvejen 8, Bellahøj, 2700 Brønshøj, tel: 38 28 97 15; fax: 38 89 02 10. Open all year. 248 beds. A

Apartments
For details of apartment accommodation in Copenhagen, contact Citilet Apartments, tel: 45-33 25 21 29; fax: 45 33 91 30 77; e-mail: citilet@citilet.dk; www.citilet.dk

---

typical hostel-type building not far from the city centre. Bus no. 2.

Danhostel Lyngby-Tårbæk Vandrerhjem, Rådvad 1, 2800 Lyngby, tel: 45 80 30 74; fax: 45 80 30 32. 1 April to 25 October. 94 beds. Small and friendly. Quite a distance from the city centre, but it is in Lyngby recreational area. S-train to Lyngby, bus to Hjortekær, and then a 15-minute walk.

CAMPING

To stay on one of Denmark's star-rated camping/caravan sites you will need to have a valid Camping Card International.

Apart from Charlottenlund, the camp sites around Copenhagen rent out cabins. These make good stand-bys in poor weather.

Bellahøj Camping, Hvidkildevej, Brønshøj, tel: 38 10 11 50; www.bellahoj-camping.dk. 1 June to 31 August. The only camp-site within easy reach of the city centre. Large grassy area with modest toilet facilities. A popular meeting place for young people in summer. Bus no. 2A.

Charlottenlund Strandpark, Strandvejen 144B, Charlottenlund, tel: 39 62 36 88. 15 May to 15 September. On the site of an old fortification. Pleasant green space right by the coast. Cramped but friendly.

Absalon Camping, Korsdalsvej 132, Rødovre, tel: 36 41 06 00; www.camping-absalom.dk. Open all year. This is a large site with enclosed pitches. Close to the E47 motorway, otherwise fine. Bus no. 6A or 123.

Tangloppen, Tangloppen 2, Ishøj Havn, tel: 43 54 07 67. 1 May to 15 September. The quietest camp site near the city centre. Located on a headland in Køge Strandpark. Bus no. 128 to Ishøj S-station.

For further information and listings, see: www.campingraadet.dk

INDEX